Photos From
Wisconsin's Past

by

Malcolm Rosholt

ROSHOLT HOUSE
Box 104
Rosholt, Wis. 54473

Foreword

In the last several years, pictures from Wisconsin's Past have been accumulating in my files and boxes, many of them gifts from friends, others I have been allowed to copy from private collections, nearly all unpublished.

After considerable procrastination, I finally decided to do another "photo album" lest these precious reminders from the past be lost or misplaced.

When the decision was made to go ahead, I remembered the collection of glass plates taken by Andrew Larson Dahl, a young immigrant from Norway to Dane County, which the State Historical Society of Wisconsin had finally acquired by an accident of history, much like many of the Mathew Brady's plates were recovered from an old hay barn in Pennsylvania. Dahl's pictures, taken in the 1870s, do not have the dramatic scenes of death and destruction to record that Brady had, but he had a unique opportunity to record a remarkable series of pictures of family life, most of them elaborately posed to emphasize the new-found status of Norwegian immigrants in this "promised land" called America. I selected more than twenty of the Dahl plates.

In addition, I searched through more than a hundred glass plates taken in the years from 1900 to 1904 by Walter Barnsdale Sr. of Plover, Wisconsin. These are given preferential treatment in a chapter devoted to the Barnsdale collection.

The chapter on Wisconsin barnstormers is not meant to be a history of aviation in Wisconsin, but the opportunity came to interview two original barnstormers, both in their mid-eighties, and rather than lose this precious information, their stories have been included in the parade of figures from Wisconsin's Past. In addition, David Jankoski of Stanley introduced me to Anne Kyle who loaned me the aviator's log book kept by her late husband, Emmett Kyle, for the years 1930-34. This is described in the same chapter.

The last chapter on logging and lumbering includes a few pictures in addition to a glossary of logging terms and a list of "firsts" in the logging industry covering a period of more than one hundred years. These pictures have accumulated since I wrote *The Wisconsin Logging Book* and *Lumbermen on the Chippewa*.

The young lady on the cover could be Wisconsin's rendition of the Gibson Girl. She is Lillian Maud Anderson, born in Scandinavia (Waupaca County), 1884, the daughter of Charles and Ida Anderson. The portrait was taken in 1906 by a transient cameraman who set up a tent on Main Street in the newly-founded village of Rosholt and stayed for a couple of days taking "studio" pictures. In 1907 Lillian Anderson married Milton Rosholt.

Malcolm Rosholt
Box 104, Rosholt, WI 54473

Library of Congress Catalog Card No.: 86-62610

ISBN: 0-910417-08-3

Printed in the United States of America by Palmer Publications Inc., Amherst, WI 54406

Contents

Family Portraits

Although family portraits were being taken in the mid-19th Century, most personal portraits were being done on ambrotypes and dagerreotypes. Family pictures were rarely taken in this way, an exception being the enlarged ambrotype which is reproduced below.

Most family portraits were taken on cameras with glass plates in the manner employed by Mathew Brady during the Civil War, and by Andrew Larson Dahl, an immigrant from Norway to Dane County in the early 1870s, whose glass plates are preserved at the State Historical Society of Wisconsin.

But in northern Wisconsin, there were few studio photographers until the 1880s when skilled technicians like William Parks of Iola were opening studios.

Where there was no local studio, commercial photographers traveled around in buggies, with black box in back containing their camera, chemicals and plates. If a family picture was taken at home, in village or farm, members gathered in front of the house usually, supported in the background by a handsome span of drivers, or a brand new Model-T Ford, symbols of a life-style better than the one enjoyed by a previous generation.

But the photographers of that period were still using a camera lens without stop-action. Usually the photographer lowered a black cloth over his head and looked through the camera to get the subjects in focus. He then inserted a glass plate into the back side of the camera and stepped forward to the side, removed the lens hood, made a silent circle that gave him an elapsed time of a second or more, and replaced the hood.

Before he waved the lens hood, the photographer cautioned everyone to remain motionless, for if they did not, a face would be blurred, and if a hand moved, this too would cause a blur. People were even warned not to smile. As a result, many of these early family pictures have a stiff, almost severe quality about them which has misled some historians to believe that they were an unhappy people, overworked probably, and too tired to smile. Far from it, our ancestors were just as anxious to tell a joke as we are, and they laughed just as hard, and on occasion they played real rough and tumble.

Around the turn of the 20th Century, people also began to have personal portraits enlarged, especially pictures of father and mother on their wedding day, or of grandfather not long before he died. These enlargements were framed and picture framers, usually the local furniture store, vied with one another in the beauty and dignity of their frames, all enclosed in heavy glass. And these pictures were hung in the family parlor, or even in the kitchen if there was no parlor, almost like religious icons. Everyone in the family knew who these people were and therefore they felt no need to write down their names. But when the last member of the family died, the heirs were often left wondering who these stern-looking people were.

A companion to the enlarged family or personal portrait was the family album, bound in covers of cloth, or leather, surrmounted by fancy metal work or even a mirror in the center. These albums were eventually filled with studio pictures of family and close friends, most of them are as sharp today as they were when taken a century ago, a rare tribute to the craftsmanship of our pioneer photographers.

The family albums shared equal space on the parlor table with the family Bible. And, lest the beauty of the photographs be marred, no one dared to write any names below. Alas, museums are today filled with albums without identification, of homeless people looking for someone to tell us who they are.

A number of photographs reproduced in this chapter are also without names, but they are of interest both because of the quality of the picture work and because the name of the studio photographer may be found at the bottom of the picture.

Not many pictures taken of any kind in Wisconsin in the 1850s survive except a few daguerreotypes and ambrotypes. One of them is this ambrotype taken in Stevens Point on the "east side" which, in 1859, probably did not extend farther east than modern Division Street. Ambrotype shows at least three people on porch, two men and woman. Both men wear frocked coats and one at left seems to be wearing black top hat. White picket fence in front was to keep out stray cattle, and white post at right was probably hitching post. Tracks in snow show in foreground. On back of ambrotype an unknown hand has written these words: "To our sisters Julia and Mary from Epha and Minnie, March 5th, 1859." Ambrotype was held by private collector who sold it in 1986 to William Paul, archivist of the Portage County Historical Society, for $100, and he donated it to the society. Photo is twice enlarged from original.

Photo, probably reproduced from a daguerreotype by Walter Barnsdale, is believed to be Lucy Whitney, daughter of Abraham Brawley who built first sawmill on Mill Creek, in 1839, where Lucy was born, allegedly the first white child in Portage County. She married Daniel Whitney and some time in the 1860s, posed for this formal studio picture. Brawley later built sawmill in Stevens Point which failed. He went off to the Civil War and was never heard of again. A street in Stevens Point preserves the memory of this pioneer.

Wedding picture of John Ciseski and Julia Glodowski. Wedding certificate states that ceremony was performed May 22, 1893, at St. Michael's church in Amherst Junction, Wisconsin, but there was no Catholic church here. The wedding was probably held at Fancher which, at the time, was served by the Amherst Junction post office. Julia, daughter of John and Krefta Glodowski, emigrants from Poland, was born in 1876, according to family tradition, in a log house situated about four miles southeast of Polonia in Portage County. The log house was rescued from oblivion and moved to the Rosholt Pioneer Museum in 1983.

Farm home of Halvor Nerison Hauge in Christiania township, Dane County, in photograph taken about 1875 by Andrew Dahl. This is one of the most imposing farm homes in Dane County and a testimony to a family of emigrants from Norway who learned quickly Yankee methods of farming, but may have had capital from Norway to take advantage of the opportunities offered to newcomers. The rectangular house is cream brick; there are brackets under the eves and small pane windows, six in each sash, with working shutters. But no storm windows for winter which made large houses like this hard to heat. The house has hip roof with hint of the Italinate style in the brackets and under the eves, and also in the verandah. Brick chimney has fancy crown. This house could have been built before 1861. Hauge is probably the tall, rough-looking character in big hat at right. Most of family members probably sit in front of fence. Others are hired hands, cooks and hired girls.

Nils Larson Dahl, a brother of photographer Andrew Dahl, poses for camera with his family at DeForest, an early Scandinavian settlement north of Madison. Mrs. Dahl displays her finest goblets, sugar bowl and tall coffee can which is probably pewter. Apples are pyramided on table and Dahl holds branch of fruit. Everyone has been told not to move but child at left, bored with all the advice, stares into space, eyes shut. Front door of house probably was never used. Black trim over doors and windows could be dry drip or beginning of porch. Mrs. Dahl has lace window curtains she probably crocheted herself. Windows, two panes to a sash, were in " modern".

This photo was taken by Andrew Dahl at Black Earth, Wisconsin, ca. 1875, probably the residence of Carlas Burton. Picture emphasizes white picket fence. Barbed wire was not yet in use and picket fencing was built around house and gardens to keep cattle out. Local ordinances governing pasturing of cattle and hogs at large were just beginning to be enforced. Milk cows often strayed from home and their owners tied bells on their necks to make them easier to find. The Burtons stand in center.

Old Settlers Club in photo taken in 1890s, probably at "Sherman's Grove," below mouth of Plover River, Stevens Point. Women wear shawls and men wear long beards. Old settlers clubs were organized throughout northern Wisconsin in 1870s, and a village as small as Ogdensburg (Waupaca County) had a club which was still holding annual picnics into the 1930s, but most clubs disbanded before WWI. At their meetings members heard papers read and story tellers recount "the good old days," all proud of their place in history, the first to arrive, or the earliest to be born on the wilderness frontier of Wisconsin.

Before the advent of the Model-T, funerals were occasions for great solemnity and piety, but none more so than when a well-known pastor died. Photo above was taken at funeral for Torger Andreas Torgerson, born in Norway, who came with his parents' family to Waupaca County in 1853 and was raised there. He served briefly as a chaplin in the Union Army before entering the ministry. After serving several congregations in Iowa, he was made president of the Iowa District of the Norwegian Synod (Lutheran), in which capacity he served until his death on January 7, 1906. Men with ruffed collars are all pastors. Under painting of Christ's Ascension is the word in Norwegian "Farvel" (farewell). The floral wreaths represent the Christian cross, an anchor, a harp, and, at the left, the inverted "horseshoe" representing the Greek Alpha, with Omega at right of cross in center of photo, both symbols of the text from Revelations 1-8 ("I am Alpha and Omega, the beginning and the ending . . . "). The open coffin with corpse stands in mid-aisle. A service like this was conducted in Norwegian, but one floral wreath at right makes a concession to the English language with the word "Rest." Deceased was a grand-uncle of the author of this photo album.

A personal picture of the deceased, surrounded by floral arrangements, was common scene at funerals after turn of the 20th Century, because photographers were able to take flashlight pictures inside Church. Enlarged studio pictures of the deceased, surrounded by floral wreaths, were also common after new photographic techniques made enlargements possible.

Jakob Aall Ottesen, an ordained pastor from Norway, emigrated to United States in 1852 and in 1860 was called to serve East and West Koshkonong churches in eastern Dane County. This picture was taken a decade before a split developed in the Norwegian Lutheran Synod over the question of predestination and other doctrines. In most congregations, if a church split occurred, the matter of church property was settled locally, but in Koshkonong, the matter was taken to court and finally to the Supreme Court of Wisconsin. Otteson refused to leave the parsonage but after four years of struggle, he accepted a call in Iowa. He is shown here in better times among family and friends at the parsonage in photo by Andrew Dahl taken about 1875. The pastor wears a hat. Others have removed their hats.

William Zeit (right) an immigrant from Switzerland, came to Medford in 1880 to open the first photography studio. He is shown here in a self-portrait with his American-born family, ca. 1895. Left, Gretchen (Mrs. Warner Smwot), Walter, Mrs. Zeit, and William Jr. Walter Zeit later taught anatomy at Marquette University.

William Zeit, Jr., and his rocking horse in picture taken in his father's studio at Medford, ca. 1900.

Photo reproduced from glass plate, probably of Klesmith family near "Smokey Spur" in southern Portage County. Without stop-action lens, photographer had to insist that everyone remain motionless.

Oscar Raymond (originally in French as Raimon), stands in back row in top hat with friends at Phillips, Wisconsin, ca. 1890. Seated in front of him is Hannah Bergman, later to become Mrs. Raymond. Two girls seated at right are Lena and Thora Torska, sisters. S.A. Johnson took picture in his studio at Phillips.

Two families probably share this log house. New settlers in southern Wisconsin, or Dane County where this picture was taken by Andrew Dahl ca. 1875, had to use black oak logs or even scrub oak when building cabin, and this one suggests that the carpenters had problems both with their logs and mortar. But the barn in background is frame. Next move this family makes will probably be into a frame house, leaving the log house for grain storage or pig house. Keeping the brush and grass down around the home place was a constant battle for these early farmers who had to use scythes, axes and wooden rakes to stay even with nature.

The strength of America is easily reflected in this straightforward picture of a couple from Waupaca, County, who went to a studio to have their picture taken, probably to send to relatives in Europe.

A lady of elegance and good taste has her picture taken, probably at a studio in Clintonville.

Viola Schmidt was confirmed at St. Anthony's Catholic church in Milwaukee. She was 13 years old when she had this picture taken in new dress, holding prayer book, one foot forward, and one arm akimbo. She later married Charles Anderson. Photo was taken at studio of N.L. Stein, 452 Mitchell Street.

Emelia (Petersen) Rasmussen, wife of Fred Rasmussen, a one-time foreman of Holt Lumber Company at Oconto, spent her spare time working on things like this, probably a table cloth or bedspread.

Easter services at Alban Lutheran Church (Portage County) April 2, 1961. Junior choir approaches from sacristy, marching past wooden cross in center aisle on way to balcony, while senior choir (not visible) will approach from vestibule in back to occupy chairs at center left. Members of the junior choir are, front to back, Paula Olson, Kari Lynn Stoltenberg, Tom Dobbe, Eric Paulson, Carol Anderson, Marie Carter, Diane Brevik, Patricia Oestreich, Vaneesa Stahl and Albert Stoltenberg. Choir marches to piano accompaniment played by Mrs. Walter Anderson, n'ee Brekke, at left, while Mark Stoltenberg, organist, waits to play for hymns. Church was built in 1878-79 and interior is fairly typical of country churches, with pulpit at right, altar in center and railing with cushion along railing for communicants to kneel at while celebrating the Holy Sacrament. At left stands baptismal font and temporary lectern. Scriptural passage beneath painting of Christ's Ascension is written in Norwegian from Corinthians 15:13. Building was later razed when congregation joined with Rosholt and Galloway to form new parish and build new church.

Winnebago Indian mother and child in photo taken at L.J. Nelson studio in Wittenberg, Wisconsin, ca. 1910. Symbol of cross on hem of skirt probably denotes that she was a Christian, but "Y" symbol is not clear.

Two unidentified pictures, (right and below) found in Milwaukee family album.

In their Easter best, two young ladies of Scandinavia pose for postcard picture taken in 1907. They are (left) Pearl Taylor and Anna Lysgen.

N. Scharff,   319 THIRD STREET, COR. PRAIRIE,
MILWAUKEE.

Brother and sister came to Scharff to have pictures taken in front of same studio prop, a make-believe rail fence. Photo was preserved in album kept by family in Milwaukee.

Boy watches baby in buggy. Milwaukee studio picture found in old family album.

The Barnsdale Collection

Walter Barnsdale Sr., born in England, went to sea as a youth and jumped ship in Canada before moving to the United States in the early 1880s where he settled in Plover, Wisconsin. He worked as a mechanic and could fix or make just about anything. After 1900 he opened a bicycle sales and repair shop, and traveled, in season, with Ringling Brothers Circus and Hagenback & Wallace where he exercised his talents as a general mechanic.

Between tours in the circus, Mr. Barnsdale became interested in the film industry and developed several devices which helped overcome the "flickers" in early films.

Around 1900 Mr. Barnsdale purchased a camera which used a glass plate, four by five inches, and in the winter of 1904 he acquired another camera which used a plate five by seven inches.

Walter and Kati Barnsdale with Eva, their first child, born in Plover in 1893.

a collector. After several years, the Barnsdale plates were acquired by Timothy Siebert, acting on behalf of the Portage County Historical Society, and they are presently preserved in the archives of the society at the Albertson Learning Resources Center of the University of Wisconsin-Stevens Point.

A representative collection of pictures from these glass plates has been made by the author. The subject material is varied and some of the pictures could easily have been used in other chapters of the present volume, but for the sake of emphasizing the rarity of the collection, the photographs are being kept together in the same chapter under the general heading of "The Barnsdale Collection."

It seems evident that in 1900 or shortly thereafter, Mr. Barnsdale

In the three or four years he was shooting "still" pictures, from 1900, it seems, down to May 1904, he amassed an impressive collection of glass plate negatives taken of people and places around the city of Plover. Many of these pictures, naturally, record his growing family after his marriage to a distant cousin, Kati Barnsdale.

For many years these glass plates were part of a collection held by the family of Walter Barnsdale Jr., but at an auction held to dispose of family heirlooms and furniture, the glass plates passed to

made a trip by train to Green Bay where he shot a few pictures, and on another occasion he took some pictures in Waupun, mainly around the state prison. Otherwise, almost all of the pictures were shot in Portage County, mainly Plover and Stevens Point and in the townships of Plover and Buena Vista.

Since none of these pictures have been published before, they form an unusual collection which depict family life at the turn of the century.

In addition to taking pictures, Mr. Barnsdale was also traveling throughout Wisconsin, down to the beginning of America's entry into World War I in 1917, showing "movies" in summer months when outdoor viewing was possible, but also in local theaters and "opera houses." His interest in the "flickers" was roused by the arrival, in 1896, of a Frenchman, probably the first to show a "movie" in Stevens Point. He was actually a magician but to attract larger audiences, he advertised a film showing.

But the French exhibitor was actually showing not a movie, as it is understood today, but a continuous series of still pictures which jumped from one to the next, hence the name "flicker," and from this probably came the expression "The flicks," a term still heard in England.

In 1897, according to Mr. Barnsdale in an interview with the Stevens Point Journal, an exhibitor came to Plover from Chicago with the first crude Edison motion picture machine which used a limelight for projecting the film frame onto a screen. But the pictures projected on the screen were small and not easy to see owing to lack of good lighting. The machine encouraged Mr. Barnsdale to build his own motion picture machine and he made several modifications which improved the quality of the film presentation. These were films, not still pictures. But he failed to enter any patents on his modifications which he blamed on the "patent scandal" of the time. In short, it was difficult for a private inventor to fight patent infringements. When Mr. Barnsdale ran his films in Chicago, he was allegedly challenged by the Edison people who could not believe that a technician from the wilderness of northern Wisconsin could have achieved some of the innovations which the Edison company was also developing to project a continuous "movie" film, not a series of slides.

By 1912, film makers were traveling around the country shooting movies, and one of them was sent by Eastman Kodak of Rochester New York, to film the story of John F. Dietz on Thornapple River in Sawyer County. The film was called "The Battle of Cameron Dam." It was exhibited in Rice Lake in 1913 and other cities and towns of northern Wisconsin, Minnesota and west to Montana. The story line of the film was strongly slanted against the big lumber companies and "trusts."

By this time, state safety regulations forced Mr. Barnsdale out of road showings and he eventually gave up his motion picture career to work for a local paper mill in Whiting-Plover.

Photo montage such as this was popular in last decades of 19th Century. This is Kati Barnsdale, 17 years old.

Boys with lunker Northern outside Warner Hotel in Plover.

Worth ("Wash") Altenburg in front of home in Plover, with niece Frances Barnsdale at his side. Photo taken May 10, 1904.

Plover chapter of Modern Woodman of the World, a fraternal organization. Members in front row hold symbolic axes, all but one in center who holds broadax.

Frank Singley, saloon keeper in Plover, riding "railroad bike" probably made by Walter Barnsdale in his bicycle and repair shop in Plover.

Walter Coddington's dredge at work on Buena Vista Marsh (Portage County).

Steam fire engine probably at Plover. Water hose lies on snow-covered ground.

Hod Warner operated this hotel at southwest corner of Post and Willow in Plover. Picture was taken when streets were flooded in early spring. Note temporary board walk in left foreground. No drainage.

Ida Warner, wife of Hod Warner, keeper of hotel in Plover.

Common type of swing was used mostly by children and by young couples. Picture was probably taken in Plover.

A Sunday school class, Plover Methodist Church, spring of 1904. Front row, l. to r.: Bea Donovan, Eva Gee, Effie Sterling, Elizabeth Barnsdale, and Maybelle Altenburg. Back, left, Bernice Pierce, Isla Warner, Frances Donovan, Mrs. Mamie Skinner (teacher), Halley Clendenning, Ellia Bahner and Eva Blisdale.

Fourth of July float passing Warner Hotel in Plover early 1900s.

Walter Barnsdale took this picture of his family in 1904 in front of house in Plover, with his wife Kati watching from porch at right. Seated in front center is Myra (Mrs. Willis Brooks), and in back, l. to r. are Emma, Elizabeth (Mrs. Albert Brown) who holds Walter Jr., George, Eva (Mrs. Daniel Hetzel) who holds Frank, and Frances (Mrs. LeRoy Gordon.).

Kids playing in snow, a perennial scene in Wisconsin, Myra, Walter, Frank and Richard Barnsdale, Richard on the sled.

Farm scene probably Buena Vista township (Portage County). Youth sits on hay mower, but this is late summer and grain stacks, barely visible through tree, wait threshing machine. Barn at left was probably for dairy cattle and barn at right for horses. Open door on second floor of barn was for hay to be pitched in by hand from hay load.

There were no lawn mowers when this picture was taken. Lady at right leads grass cutting with scythe while her partner handles wooden rake. Most families in small communities had barn back of house where a milk cow and a pair of drivers were kept. Small windows on barn are manure holes, built small to keep out cold in winter.

Sign over door in center reads: "Weber Wagons" but location of picture uncertain.

Potato picking time in Portage County. Man third from left sits on digger pulled by three horses. Others are pickers and box handlers. Wooden crated boxes hold sixty pounds of potatoes and were most efficient for handling and lifting. Pickers moved boxes along row of potatoes as they moved forward, and handlers lifted boxes unto wagon to be hauled to farm storage, usually in basement or cellar of house. But much of potato crop at this time was hauled directly off field into town and sold to brokers for cash.

Threshing scene probably from Buena Vista township (Portage County). Steam engine stands at left, belt running between grain stacks all the way to separator at right. Long belt increased power. Separator boss stands atop his machine on lookout for trouble. Straw blower reaches over stack at right, team and wagon haul grain sacks to granary.

Fun time in Plover. Barn at left was probably home base for donkey in cart shaft.

31

Sign over door reads: "Plover Post Hall." Building stood in Plover, Wisconsin, and was meeting place for veterans of the Civil War who had joined the Grand Army of the Republic, a veterans organization founded in 1866. This small group probably represents the last of their number in Plover, and their last group picture.

Plover elementary school stood north of Plover village and also served township. Picture was taken by Barnsdale in 1904.

Plover Methodist church as it looked about 1900. Green Bay & Western Rail Road tracks run in foreground and sign over road reads: "Watch out for the cars." Church is presently being restored as museum sponsored by Portage County Historical Society.

Stevens Point Normal School, 1904, east Main Street in foreground.

Below: Photo from Clark Street Bridge on Wisconsin River in Stevens Point, with train of Green Bay & Western Rail Road approaching depot (not visible at left). Beyond looms tower of Denver Hotel, and at left is close-up of hotel which faced Clark Street at northeast corner of Third Street. Name of hotel later changed to "Commercial." Mansart roof was architectural favorite in late 19th Century, an import from France. Bay window at corner designates lobby, and steps at center no doubt led to reception desk. Poles at right are probably telephone and electric light. Note lamp (upper left) over street intersection. Lumber wagon (left) stands at curb.

Main Street in Plover, Wisconsin, probably looking south. In center of road in distance farmer leaves with two big milk cans. At right are hitching posts for horses, and a pump for drinking water.

Two Plover belles at the piano. Sheet music at left: "I Wonder How the Old Folks Are At Home," and other, "Let Me Call You Sweetheart." Number at lower right is photographer's imprint on glass negative, probably for file purposes.

Ski meet in progress at hill overlooking Plover River in Stevens Point, presently part of Iverson Park. Picture taken in 1904.

Fishing for trout was fun in old days, no bag limit, no size limit. These two boys used manufactured poles with small reel.

Banner reads: "Division of Wisconsin Sons of Veterans, U.S.A. Organized 1884." This was national organization of young people, all children of Union Army veterans of the Civil War. It was mainly a social organization to perpetuate the memories of their fathers' participation in the war and to get together for oyster stew and dancing. Barnsdale took picture at height of Spanish-American war hysteria, and men all wear campaign hats which were regulation issue for Spanish-American war troops. Four hold rifles in "order arms" position. Rifles could be National Guard issue. Man at left, holding sword, poses as officer. Elderly men reclining in front of women are Civil War veterans. There were at least two chapters of this organization in Portage County, one in Belmont township where members met at Blaine community hall, and one at Plover which met at G.A.R. hall. This was perhaps last group picture taken. The "sons" were now grown men like their fathers before them.

This may be early form of skeet shooting but movement of hand on man at right blurs what could be a clay pigeon he throws into the air. But this is posed picture. No one would stand this close to the shooter.

Section crew on hand pumper passing through Plover on Green Bay & Western Rail Road tracks.

Simon A. Sherman, pioneer lumberman to Stevens Point, built sawmill below mouth of Plover River and excavated a canal between the Plover and the Wisconsin River which acted as a flume to float logs into his mill complex. People referred to it as "Sherman's cut" but nothing remains of the canal today except for this rare picture from the Barnsdale Collection. Men watch photographer from atop dam in distance.

Family of A. Sherman in photo taken on May 4, 1904 in front of house now made into restaurant at Plover.

Lakeboats tied up for the season at Green Bay. At left the "Eugene C. Hart" Green Bay and Mackinac service, and below, boat at left called at Sturgeon Bay, Menomonee, Marinette and Escanaba. Boats appear to be frozen in snow-covered ice.

In 1813, an American naval task force, under Commodore Oliver Hazard Perry, defeated an English fleet on Lake Erie which forever halted the advance of the British into the Western states. Perry's flagship, the *Niagara,* later fell into neglect and sank in the mud at Misery Bay, Erie, Pennsylvania. In 1912-13 the United States Navy allocated funds to raise the ship and restore it, and in July 1913, it set sail on a visit to Great Lakes ports to celebrate the 100th anniversary of Perry's victory. Among the cities visited was Green Bay which set aside August 10 to 16 as "Perry's Victory Centennial, Green Bay Homecoming." The flagship docked at the foot of Pine Street on Fox River and invited visitors to come aboard. Among them were these two gentlemen from Plover, Wisconsin, Dr. George Whiteside and Morton Skinner.

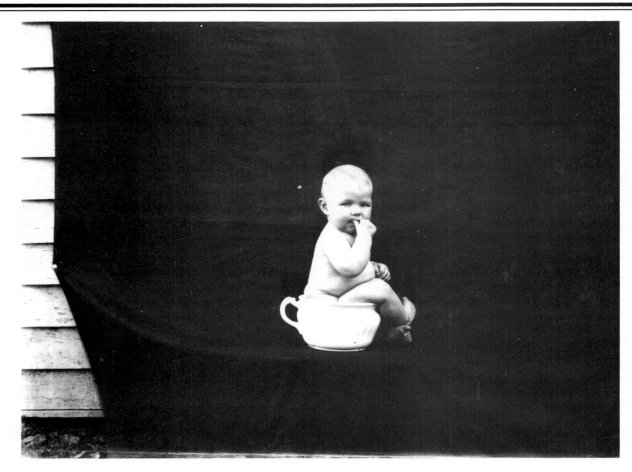

First I go pottee . . .

Then I have my bath
. . . and my name is
Myra and I had my pit-
cher took in 1900, I tink.

Circumstantial evidence suggests that Walter Barnsdale did not have a studio with a backdrop shown here. He may have copied the picture from a commercial photographer who, in common with others, often posed actresses in theatrical costumes and attitudes. But the glass plate this is taken from is badly faded.

Family of Paul Koshellek in picture taken at Plover in 1904.

The Postcard Fad

For hundreds of years, people who wished to write or correspond with distant relatives, friends and business associates sat down to write a letter ("I take pen in hand") on a piece of stationary and enclosed it in an envelope.

In the 1890s someone in Europe came up with a new method of correspondence—the postcard, often called the "penny postcard" because it required only a one-cent stamp. The postcard took advantage of new techiques in photography and printing in which scenic views were printed on one side of a card, measuring three and a half inches by five and a half inches, while the opposite side was reserved for name, address and message. These cards were produced by the millions and in the early years they could be purchased at stationary stores or, in small villages, at the local drug store.

Taking pictures for postcards became an overnight success and the craze spread across the Atlantic to the United States and Canada in the early 1900s. For some reason, few cards before 1908 can be found, but after that date, the country was deluged with postcards, many of them shot by expert photographers who used good chemicals in the processing of their pictures. As a result, many cards can still be found which have retained, after seventy-five years, their original sharp quality. James Parfitt of Tigerton and James Colby of Wausau took scores of postcard pictures of the logging woods and of old depots, most of them are remarkable for their clarity and depth of focus.

The first use of postcards in the U.S. may have started in 1901 by photographers at Coney Island and at summer resorts on the Maine Cost. In 1902 Eastman Kodak began to provide paper with "postcard" printed on the back, and in May 1903, the first Kodak cameras for this size, the No. 3A Folding Pocket Kodak, came on the market. It was an instant success.

Eastman Kodak offered postcards in four types of paper in 1904. The peak year in the trade was 1911 when nine types of emulsions were put on the market, including blueprint postcards.

But any camera which made a larger image than the postcard, such as a five by seven camera, could be used. The earliest postcard in the collection included here was taken in Milwaukee and is stamped December 10, 1905 at 10 p.m. It is also tinted. In fact, tinted postcards were introduced earlier that same year, and from then on, all kinds of tinting and exotic postcards were manufactured, not to mention montages with airplanes flying over Wittenberg, Wisconsin, and street cars in villages which never had a street car, much less an airplane. In addition, humorous picture-cards were made with witty cliches, people, and caricatures.

Glass plates, like Mathew Brady used in the Civil War, continued to be used by some photographers right down to the beginning of World War II, and there were even glass plate cameras for amateurs made in the postcard size. But the introduction of the 3A Graflex camera made it possible to fit the lenses with the best available, including the F/4.5 Zeiss Tessar.

Even the folding pocket Kodak camera produced sharp and detailed negatives, and as these were printed by contact, all the detail was preserved. The 3A negative has about twelve times the area of a 35mm. negative.

The *Ladies Home Journal,* dated April 1900, (which sold for ten cents), carries an advertisement featuring the catch-phrase, "The Witchery of Kodakery," a period when Kodak cameras were selling in several sizes priced at five to thirty-five dollars.

Included in the following chapter are four pages of color postcards celebrating different seasons of the year mostly, a rare collection, nostalgia compounded.

One of the most oft written lines on a "penny" postcard are the words: "How are you? I am fine. I hope you are the same." Most correspondents had a touch of writer's cramps and confined themselves to a few words even though there was room for more on the card. Below follow a few messages taken from some cards in the author's collection, the first one from a lady in Manawa to her son who worked in Rosholt, stamped 1909:

"Dear——. We are looking for you to come home every day. We have some pigs for you to kill when you get here. I was down to New London yesterday. Made a pretty good thing of it. It's nice to be in a business. I got my fare paid and about a dollar over. Come home as soon as you can. John came out ahead in the lawsuit." Later (on top of card): "Pa has sold the pigs alive."

where we are staying the Blatz

Coming home tomorrow

Are having a fine time.
All saw Messiah.

One of earliest postcards made in Wisconsin taken in front of City Hall in Milwaukee. Well dressed people strolling on street have probably been hired by photographer to pose. Writer says he/or she have been staying at the Blatz Hotel. Card also has room for message at bottom as well as on opposite side. It is stamped Milwaukee, December 28, 1905.

Another written in 1909: "Dear Brother. This is the second Easter card I have sent you. Try and come home for Easter. Pa is splitting wood. Ma wants you to get a souvenir from Rosholt. She will pay you. I have a new sheet of music. It's all the rage now."

Here's one from Milwaukee to a friend in Iola: "Hello there. Say you did keep your promise did you not? That view of Upper Main street (in Iola) is fine and hope there will be a day coming when I may view it with my own eyes. I spent Sunday at the place on the other side of this card (Whitefish Bay). Fine time. When shall we three meet again, Lovingly, B.M.R."

This one from Milwaukee to a girl in Oshkosh: "Hello . . . received your postal. Very glad to hear from you, as you are rather busy. Yes, so am I. I suppose you like the city. Have you been to any dances since you were in Iola. Wasn't that a great dance we had. Haven't heard from Alfred P."

One card merely gives the address of the person it was sent to without any message, but the opposite side of the card says, "Greetings from Rosholt, WI." and that apparently was enough.

Yours in haste

Grand Avenue Boulevard, Milwaukee 1909.

Boat House, Humbolt Park, Milwaukee 1908.

Whitefish Bay 1911.

2283

Enlarged postcard of Plankinton House, the leading hostelry in Milwaukee of the 19th Century, on Grand (now Wisconsin) Avenue. Signs over entrance to lobby read: "Plankinton House, Grand Avenue Lunch Room." Postcard was made in Germany for A.C. Bosselman & Company of New York, and it is stamped Milwaukee post office October 12, 10 P.M. 1909, addressed to a lady at 262 Scott Street in Oshkosh.

Dam at Milwaukee River from postcard stamped Milwaukee March 19, 1909.

45

8232. Coming to Sheboygan, Wis.

Postcard is stamped 1914 and caption atop card reads: "Coming to Sheboygan, Wis."

1317 — Pier Light, Sheboygan, Wis.

Enlarged postcard picture of Pier Lighthouse at Sheboygan, stamped April 9, 1910, same year as construction began on new light which also eliminated bridge walk at left. Main lighthouse today stands on North Pier.

Litho-Chromse post-card made in Germany. Card is stamped Waupaca July 19, 1907 and scene is of Main Street in Waupaca looking north.

High School in New London from undated postcard.

Canal at Portage linking Wisconsin River (in distance) and Fox River. From undated postcard.

Graded School, Iola Wis,

The Home of the Green Bay Business College.

St. Mary's Hospital, Oshkosh, Wis.

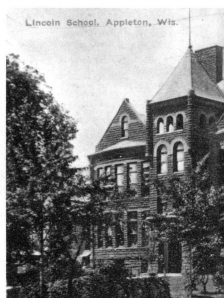

Lincoln School, Appleton, Wis.

Oconto County Court House, Oconto, Wis. Pub. for A. H. Luckenbach, Druggist.

GRAFTON HALL, FOND DU LAC, WIS.
6751

Northwestern Depot, Oshkosh, Wis.

Court House, Waupaca, Wis.

Main Building, Lawrence College, from postcard stamped Appleton 1908.

Lawrence Street Bridge across Fox River at Appleton, St. Joseph's church and school in distance. Postcard stamped 1911.

Where Omro people take their vacation. Postcard stamped 1909.

A Merry X Mas

hristmas ★
ad Christmas
sweet herald
f good-will

A Peaceful Hearth

A heart where Peace has part:
A hearth where joys abound:
So may your hearth and heart
By every Yule be found!

S.K.Cowan

A Merry Christmas.

Greetings From Rosholt Wis.

A Happy New Year to You

Best Wishes

A Merry Christmas to you

TO GREET YOU

In the desert a fountain is springing,
In the wild waste there still is a tree,
And a flower in the old garden blooming
That speaks to my spirit of thee.

A HAPPY EASTER

If wishes could make you happy,
I'd wish and wish so hard,
'Twould make you the happiest thing
alive
The minute you get this card.

Spoofs and humor were part of postcard fad. At left, heavily armed hunters, bag rabbit big enough to be carried on pole. Below, caption reads: "What the future may bring to Wittenberg," i.e. a Curtiss pusher (upper left) and probably a June Bug (upper center), and streetcar, all montages. Sign at right reads: "Netzel & Vandaree, General Merchandise" and at left "White Hotel." View looks north on Main Street.

Pioneer Farms and Farmers

An old account book kept by the first storekeeper in the village of Scandinavia (Waupaca County) in 1852-55 shows that the new settlers to this area were bringing homemade butter to the store to exchange for groceries or for credit on their charge account.

The fact that butter was being made at home on the farm—usually by the housewife—means that the farmer had a milk cow, probably two cows, but seldom three. Dairying was in its infancy. There were no cheese factories or creameries to bring milk to for making cheese or butter. Yet, less than twenty-five years later, dairy herds in Wisconsin had expanded. The 1876 plat of Portage County reveals that this far north in Wisconsin, scarcely settled, there was already a cheese factory in Buena Vista township.

The making of cheese was something most of the immigrant farmers from Europe, as well as the Yankees, knew something about and, from the evidence of photographs taken by Andrew Larson Dahl in Dane County in the 1870s, it seems obvious that dairying had become an important factor in the economy of southern Wisconsin within one generation.

Observe Dahl's pictures, for example, of cattle standing in the barnyard. They are not purebreds. They are a nondescript breed of cows with no bloodline. In short, most are "scrubs." It took time for the farmers to realize that a bad bull begat cows which produced milk with a low butter fat content. Yet, these scrubs ate as much as the cows that produced a higher butter fat. Thus the race for purebreds began, and by the 1890s, certain farmers were taking the lead in developing herds of pure-bred Holsteins and Guernseys.

But, while some dairy farmers forged ahead, others lagged behind, either because they lacked the capital to buy a good bull, or because they did not realize what genetic research had already proved, namely, that good bulls produce good heifer calves that become high fat producers.

In the 1840s and 1850s, in Wisconsin, most farmers among the German settlements around New Glarus, and the Norwegian settlement around Koshkonong, were mainly into wheat growing, and this continued to be the leading cash crop until the early 1870s when wheat growing began to be phased out, not because there was no market, but because many farmers had not realized that they must use fertilizer and follow a crop rotation program.

Some early farmers in southern Wisconsin raised tobacco. Profit could be made from small acreages, but not everyone knew how to grow tobacco any more than some farmers in Marathon County knew how to raise ginseng, a root favored by Chinese medicine men. Most of the early farmers who tried growing ginseng failed, probably because they had not learned how to nurture the plant, one of the most touchy ever grown in Wisconsin.

The account book kept at the first store in Scandinavia shows that some farmers were raising oats and rye, as well as wheat. There is no mention of alfalfa or clover.

One cash crop that required little acreage was hops, the dried ripe cones of the female flower used in the brewing of beer. Farmers as far north as Marathon County were raising hops, and the hops culture continued past the turn of the 20th Century before it was phased out.

From this, it seems clear that pioneer farming in Wisconsin was a varied experience. Some farmers raised tobacco, some grain, some lived by dairying, and some made extra cash raising hops, apples, bees and tapping maple sugar.

But no matter how hard they tried, not all farmers were suited to farming. Thousands of immigrants from Europe came to America on the promise of free land, that is, after the Homestead Act was passed by Congres in 1862, but a majority of those who took out homestead claims, failed, and moved back to villages or cities to work in other trades or to enter into business. It seemed like a process of natural selection: to the fittest belonged the land.

Before irrigation, farming was always a gamble, a gamble with the weather man, with the banker and with the land itself. Many farmers who came out of Chicago into Northern Wisconsin were lured by the promise of "cheap land" in the former timber belts of Price County, or in the sand hills of Waushara County, only to learn that this land was not suited to agriculture as it was then practiced, meaning without irrigation. These farmers failed because no matter how hard they tried, they could not raise crops to match the work

Photograph by Andrew Dahl, ca. 1875, taken on a farm in Dane County among Norwegian newcomers who have already struck deep roots in America and in the American dream. Vehicle at right is two-seated light wagon. Dahl seems to have experimented with new art form in photography, spreading his subjects across the foreground in different poses and attitudes. Two men at left make believe they are conversing. Man reclining with feet out (center) sits on *kubbestole*, a Norwegian chair carved out of log butt, usually basswood or pine. Windows have working shutters, and ferns and climbing vines festoon porch.

and expense of putting them in.

Newspaper accounts in the late 1930s and early 1940s reveal that farmers were in trouble and auction posters were common, mostly as a result of the dry years of the 1930s. With the diversification which characterized farming in Wisconsin, counties most cruelly hit by the drought of 1935-36 might have survived without government feed loans, but there was no cure for a drought, no matter how diversified the farmer. And then the wind began to blow in the Dakotas and down to Kansas and across Oklahoma and out of the wind came the "Oakies" and the fence lines buried in dust and sand. In North Dakota one farmer was heard to say that it was too bad that the Depres-

sion came right during the Hard Times!

Urban viewers of the farm scene often believe that people on farms a century ago lived a simple life, without complexities but this may be classified as a myth. Take the case of a farmer in Waupaca County whose hay was ready to be cut but the scythe needed sharpening and he had no grindstone. He would have to go to a relative miles away. The farmer had a wife and baby, and a cow. The wife would not stay home alone because her husband would have to be gone overnight. To resolve this impasse, the farmer decided to take his family along, wife and child in the wagon, the cow tethered behind, all for the want of a grindstone.

Farm house photographed by Andrew Dahl, Dane County, ca. 1875. Man at left sits on sulky and is probably driving a stud horse. The usual fee for stud service in late 19th and early 20th Century was $5 "foul on side," that is, if mare did not foul, stud fee was returned to her owner. At right, youth sits on machine, probably hay mower.

House of cream brick in Springfield township, Dane County, photographed by Andrew Dahl, ca. 1875. Windmill at right probably was manufactured in Batavia, Illinois. Girl at right reclines in theatrical manner. Man in white shirt sleeve (center) seems to hold corn stalks, probably to show how tall the corn has grown under his management.

Raising hops, which were used in making of beer, was an important cash crop among Wisconsin farmers in last decades of 19th Century. It was grown all over southern Wisconsin and as far north as Portage County. Hop seed was planted in ground and after growing two or three feet, the vine was attached to tall pole dug into ground, and what appears in picture as tall trees in background are actually hop vines clinging to their poles. Men usually cut poles down and carried vines to big open boxes where teenagers, all girls, plucked hop pods off the vines and tossed them into the big box. Hop pickers lived in special quarters on some farms and moved from one to the next. At the end of season, hop festivals were staged at which time there was dancing and fun. Ladies in picture at left and right are in formal gown, all part of the festival, but everyone crowned with clusters of hop pods. Two youths reclining in center wear tall black hats as part of the fantasy.

Andrew Dahl took picture above, of tobacco field with grain stacks in distance, next to barn, ca. 1875. He then moved in for close-up shot of same stacks, all neatly capped and sloped to shed water. Stackers took pride in perfect symmetry and sharpness of peak. Board fence runs around stacks to keep cattle out until threshing time. Produce suggests this farmer was both in dairying and in tobacco. Shed at right was probably for drying tobacco leaves.

Manufacturer's mark on arm of windmill is blurred but the name "Illinois" can be made out, probably where it was manufactured. Building a framework around the base of the windmill was not uncommon. An early farm near Iola (Waupaca County) had one similar to this although not as tall. The enclosed windmill may have been favored by some farmers because it offered protection against rain and snow when the farmer was adjusting the pipes to the water tank for the cattle or when pumping water for the house. Building in center of picture is probably for storage as well as a place for drying tobacco leaves, or hop pods. Andrew Dahl took picture, ca. 1875.

Michalson's blacksmith and machine shop in Argyle, Wisconsin, photographed by Andrew Dahl, ca. 1875. Mold-board plow in foreground has steel, curved beam, and one in back has long, traditional wood beam, probably hickory. Both plows have been given coat of paint with fancy decorations. At left of shop stands light wagon, high-wheeled with narrow rims.

Unidentified barnyard, Dane County, photographed by Andrew Dahl, ca. 1875. Impressive cupola is crowned by a spread eagle weather vane. Louvers allow dampness from hay to escape. Horse barn appears to be at left and dutch doors suggest cattle barn. Man in center stands next to open door. Close-up shows door littered with manure, probably from the sheep which are barely visible at right. Lean-to shed was also used for grain storage and tools. Cows in foreground seem to be wading knee deep in manure, and white horse at left is in need of a curry-comb.

Down to the end of the 19th Century, a device found on many farms was the shaving bench, more often referred to by its German name, "schnitzlebenk." Shown here is Peter Weiler who made this one for the Rosholt Pioneer Museum. By keeping his feet firmly on the peddle, he holds stick in vise to use drawshave. Clamp could swing forward or backward and could hold a piece of leather or a shake shingle as well. The standard 18-inch shake needed to be thinned at one end and this was the tool to do it. Photo taken near Park Falls by the author in 1985.

John and Gunhild Swenson emigrated from Vegarshei, Norway and settled on a farm in New Hope township (Portage County). Buildings, both house and barn are frame. The Swensons stand at left flanked at right by Ida, Thomas, Andrew, Perry and Daniel. The latter holds Perry with one hand and colt with the other. He is probably wearing vest brought from Norway. Beyond fence at left is son Olaf who holds reins on horse. Picture was taken ca. 1892.

Farm buildings of Ole P. Dobbe in Section 13, town of Alban (Portage County). First part of barn (near end) was built in 1902 and far end later. House on hill at left was built in 1903. Log building formerly stood on Baily Creek and was moved to new site where it was used for milk house where cream separator stood, and for blacksmith shop (near end). Horse entered door next to window to be shod. Windmill was erected about 1910. Frame work was built on ground and fan attached to frame and entire structure raised with block and tackle anchored to pine tree. Building on other side of windmill is woodshed. In center is granary, middle section for grain storage, right side (door open) for wagon and buggy, and left side for binder and hay mower. Barely visible under eve of barn is stave silo, later raised several feet higher. Lean-to on barn was first used for cattle, but later remodelled for horse barn with cement floor. Cattle then occupied near end of barn and hay mow the far end. Tract of 130½ acres of cut-over land was cleared by Dobbe and family, but there was no room to expand and in 1931 he gave up farming. Land was purchased by neighbors and buildings razed. Transient cameraman took picture in March 1918.

Farm of Tollef Gjermandson, a Norwegian newcomer in Pleasant Springs township, Dane County. In one generation this immigrant has built big barn and raised herd of cattle. Entrance to cattle barn seems to be through gothic openings below windows at left, and entrance to horse barn is at upper right. Hay was brought into loft from opposite side of barn. Breed of cattle is mixed, most of cows probably "scrubs," and not big milk producers. But this picture by Andrew Dahl, ca. 1875, shows beginning of big dairy herds in Wisconsin. Cheese factories were being built everywhere. 1876 plat of Portage County shows one in Buena Vista township. Fencing around barnyard is makeshift, of cull lumber. Barbed wire had yet to be invented. Straw stack at upper right suggests picture taken in early fall.

A barn-raising bee was both a social event and an economic necessity. When a farmer was planning to abandon an old log barn and build a frame barn, he engaged the local sawmill to furnish timbers and lumber which were hauled to the site of construction where the framework was prefabricated on the ground and then lifted, pulled, pushed into place, and held together with pegs bored through sockets made by large augers. The families of the workers brought baskets of food and liquids along, and the children exchanged games. This picture from Dane County, taken by Andrew Dahl, ca. 1875, is one of the earliest extant on a barn raising in Wisconsin. This type of bee, inherited from the eastern states, was largely discontinued by 1915.

Andrew Dahl took pictures almost entirely of Norwegian immigrant families and their farms. Norwegian-born himself, he was at ease among his countrymen. The owner of this farm has come out in field to show how his reaper-mower works, but the men are all in white shirts. This is not a binder (yet to be invented). Man behind the driver has wooden fork which he rakes grain off platform on reaper into small piles. These were raked together by man at left and tied into shocks. Instead of twine, the shocker picked three or four strands of grain which he tied around the shock and made a loop to secure it, an art long lost to later generations. Man at right holds cradle scythe which he probably uses to cut around corners where reaper can not go. Gabled upright and wing house in distance is probably most common type of houses built in late 19th and early decades of the 20th Century Wisconsin. Kitchen was usually in the wing.

Lady gathers muskmelons, probably on farm in Buena Vista township, Portage County, ca. 1900.

Potato digger, probably used on farm in Buena Vista township, Portage County, 1900. On this model, wheels in front were adjusted for depth of shovel that scooped up potato hills. "Shaker" in back was rigid. In later models shaker could be adjusted in event vines were wet or potatoes muddy. Instead of wheels in front of shovel, later models had hard rubber roller, about same size as the wheels, which fit between the bar and pushed potato vines down. Wheels on this digger have cletes and there was little improvement on cletes. Beam in front of digger had hook for evener which was hitched to team of horses, or two teams, according to ground conditions and stones.

Successful farmer near Knowlton (Marathon County), early 1900s. Family displays fruit of the harvest.

Light sleigh and team struggling through new snow on streets of Plover, ca. 1900.

Photo from 1920s shows farmer on tractor with iron wheels and cleats pulling stone boat. This method of picking up stones was one of most common in Wisconsin. Two men could roll fairly large stone unto stone boat. But this farmer is not hauling farther than he has to. Note stone pile in distance at left. Picture was taken near Rib Lake. Tractor ran on kerosene.

By the 1870s, cheese factories were being built throughout southern Wisconsin and as far north as the town of Buena Vista (Portage County). As the dairy herds grew in the 1890s, creameries were spotted here and there to make butter. In photo above is cheese factory at "Little Chicago" (northwest of Wausau), ca. 1910. Factory was probably at left, and cheesemaker's house at right. (Right), a creamery at Ellis, town of Sharon, (Portage County). Farmers all seemed to arrive with milk cans at same time, the better to exchange news and swap stories. (Below), a "skimming station" at North Star, town of Sharon (Portage County), ca. 1907. Skimming stations were located in areas where there was not large enough dairy herds to support either cheese factory or creamery. Operator Gorecki skimmed the whole milk and hauled the cream to nearest creamery, probably at Ellis.—Photos reproduced by special permission of Scott McCormick.

Fun and Recreation

Fun and recreation in the early decades of settlement in Wisconsin was arranged mostly at the local level. Organized sports were practically unheard of except for a few professional baseball teams which most people heard about but never saw because they played only in big cities, mostly in the east.

Football and basektball teams were being organized in Normal Schools in the 1890s, and by the early 1900s high school and parochial schools on the academy level competed against each other in baseball and basketball.

"City teams," both in basketball and football, were also organized at this time, but the number of games actually played was limited, one team visiting another was often forced to ride on a railroad handcar over the local branch line of the Wisconsin Central or Chicago & North Western railroads.

Basketball was often played in a hall built originally for roller skating, and the baskets were so close to the ceiling that it was nearly impossible to loop the ball. It had to be banked in and as a result, basketball scores were low and defense was the name of the game.

Roller skating was probably the most popular indoor sport in the 1890s and early 1900s, and rinks, which also served as basketball courts, dance halls, and other community affairs, were built in many towns.

As for other entertainment, aside from sports events, nearly every village and town in Wisconsin had its own bandstand where the local cornet band gave concerts on the 4th of July, or on Saturday evenings to local townspeople and farmers.

In the 1880s, a new movement, aimed at entertainment and enlightenment, originated in Chautauqua, New York state. Entertainers, concert artists, public speakers and dramatic troupes performed in tents. These tents were not moved every night like the circus. Instead, several towns contracted with agents of the Chautauqua company to sponsor these events, and six or seven sponsors were engaged to guarantee a program for every night for one week. The performers traveled by horse team and train in the 1890s, and the 1900s by train and the Model-T Ford truck, or car. After a week the tents came down and were moved to new locations.

Drama on the Chautauqua circuit was mostly comedy mixed with melodrama, one of the favorites, of course, the long running New York hit "Puddin' Head Wilson." The players carried their own wardrobe in trunks which had to be hauled from one town to the next. Local sponsors found volunteers to help in this and to sell tickets and provide ushers. The gate was assured; season tickets were sold in advance.

The name Chautauqua and all that it once meant to the small towns of America is now all but forgotten and one has to be quite old (like the author) to remember the Chautauqua.

In winter time, public lyceum courses were sponsored in rural areas as well as cities. Artists, speakers and musicians performed in the local "opera house" or in school gymnasiums and churches, any place large enough—and warm enough—to hold an audience.

These lyceums and Chautauqua were not sponsored as money-making affairs. They were cultural events which filled a deep need, especially among the rural communities of America, most of whom could not afford to pay top fees commanded by such speakers as Mark Twain or artists like Jenny Lind.

The perennial home talent plays were used to make money for the community. Farces and negro ministral shows, performed by white men in black face, became popular throughout Wisconsin.

And then there was the circus which came to town. This was always a high point of the summer season.

But probably the most popular form of entertainment from the 1890s to the mid-1920s, was public dancing. People, young and old, got together to dance, sometimes all night. Dancing was frowned on by some church authorities, and local dances were often held in private homes to avoid censor from the local pastor. But after 1900 church taboos against public dancing were overcome. A 4th of July dance, for example, was held in a new planing mill in the village of Rosholt because a new floor had been laid and the machinery not yet installed, and when a new barn was built it was often used for a dance before haying time.

Most communities had a dance hall either in town or out by a lake or on a river, and people

Frank Leahy (right), head coach at Notre Dame, fries trout while Frederick C. Miller (center) and two sons, Frederick Jr. (left) and Carl, and third man, not identified, look on. Fishing party was given special permit to fish on Menomonee Indian Reservation where this picture was taken in 1953. On December 17, 1954, Frederick Sr. and Frederick Jr. were both killed in crash of private airplane.

drove their buggies, or their new cars to these resorts and spent the night dancing.

Going to the movies in the years between 1910 and 1925 was an occasional affair. M.L. Hite who operated a butcher shop in Rosholt, also built a public hall where occasional dances were held and, by 1916, he had installed a 35 mm. motion picture machine (arc light and hand cranked). Silent movies were shown once a week, usually Saturday night, most of them Westerns starring William S. Hart and Harry Cary. Added input was provided by a local boy or girl who played a player piano, accenting dramatic scenes with piano fortisimo. The novelty of seeing people move on screen held the interest of the audience, not the story line. But there were exceptions, such as "Birth of a Nation." "Broken Blossoms," and "When Knighthood was in Flower."

Phillips football team was playing Glidden, ca. 1915. Players in back-field wear rubber nose protector which they put over nose when smashing off tackle. Nose protector was held secure by a an extension that fit between the front teeth of the player. This equipment was used in 1890s and early 1900s before it was realized that more teeth were broken than noses smashed in scrimmage. Real estate broker uses wall of his office to advertise "timber lands" for sale, meaning cut-over lands.

Stevens Point High School's Wisconsin Valley Football Champions, season of 1926. Photo taken on lot presently occupied by skating rink east of P.J. Jacobs Junior High School and view looks south to Main Street which runs east and west. Linemen, left to right, Albert Neuberger, end, Harold Fors, tackle, Harry Eichman, guard, Joe Siebert, center, Richard Barnsdale, guard, Mike Smith, tackle and Alfred Tierny, end. In backfield, l. to r., George Anderson, halfback, Forrest McDonald, fullback, Kenneth Fishleigh, quarterback, and Bernard Gussel, halfback. Standing, l. to r., John Rellahan, business manager, Douglas Mainland, Frank Bogaczyk, Robert Pollard, Emil Pagel, Lloyd Bidwell, Alex Eichman, Alois Razner, George Courtwright, Glen Pike, and Walter Hunting, coach. Next right, Everett Bright, Gordon Copps, Verne Somers, Glen White, Robert Spindler, Sam Block, Francis O'Brien, Robert Betlach, Edwin Somers, and Dr. E.H. Rogers.

Before indoor rinks were completed this is the way young hockey players got their start in life, out on the ice where nature made it, this rink is on Cashin's Creek running into the Plover. One of goalies seems to be crouched for action in upper center, and man in white pants may be referee. Note muskrat house at center right. Photographer Howard Clark shot picture in 1936.

Agricultural Contest, Wis. Banker's Ass'n, Wittenberg Wis. 12/11-12.

In 1912 there was a competition under way for the best minstrel show in Wisconsin, sponsored by the Wisconsin Banker's Association. This picture was taken of the Wittenberg show on December 11, 1912. The white men in black face are all local business men with "Mr. Interloctor" on the high chair in center. At the two ends, left and right, the men holding the tamborines were the "end men," one called "Mr. Bones" and the other "Mr. Tambo." The program included jokes between the Mr. Interloctor and the end men, interspersed with songs and music from the troupe and orchestra. The second part of the performance included skits by all members and ended with the "hoedown" or "walk-around" in which each member did his own thing while others sang and clapped and the end men banged their tambourines. Agnes Schlytter, down in front, was piano accompaniest and Eric Onstad, orchestra leader.

When word reached Phillips in October 1910 that a big posse was preparing to lay seige to the log cabin of John F. Dietz, ''defender of Cameron Dam'' on Thornapple River, these local business men deputized each other, grabbed their rifles and prepared to join in the festivities. Left to right, George Chamberlain, Citizens Bank, Ed Neef, owner of candy store in background, and Charles Tobey, real estate dealer. Fourth man holding poster not identified. Photo preserved by Walter Raymond.

Sunday afternoon excursion on the Stanley, Merrill & Phillips Rail Road, ca. 1915.

Siwell Bowen in surrey taken at Kent (now a ghost town) in Langlade County. Using a pair of mules for drivers was uncommon sight in Wisconsin but this surrey was probably used on star route to carry mail.

Elcho baseball team in 1914. Front row, l. to r.: Bill Daga, Nick Visser, H. Weaver, and Ernest Ward; back, left, George Brandt, Rothgas Borger, John Schuh, Bernard Follstyd (manager) J. Robinson, C. Congleton, and G. Beard.

Man in top buggy, most common vehicle for "getting around" in pre-Model-T days. Picture came from a family near Knowlton (south of Mosinee).

Five piece orchestras such as this one were being organized in most small towns in the early 1900s, this one at Withee. Left to right, John Laneville, Billiam Conrad, Felix Doephner, and August Bruchart. Last not identified. Anderson Studio at Withee took picture postcard, ca. 1915.

A Bush single seater in photo probably taken near Rosholt. License plate No. 1282 for year 1915.

Steamer ''Capitol La Crosse'' was once a popular excursion boat sailing between cities of the Mississippi River from St. Louis to St. Paul. Note fancy grill work along gunwales and gaudy wheel house behind the two stacks. But davits hold only three life boats on port side, two missing.

Photographer Andrew Dahl, on horseback, had this self-portrait taken, ca. 1875, in front of Wisconsin capitol building as seen from East Washington Street in Madison. Telegraph wires run across photograph left to right at dome level. Horse is probably same Dahl used in harness on converted light wagon which he carried photographic materials, chemicals and glass plates used in developing pictures before he changed careers and became a candidate for the Lutheran ministry.

Trout hatchery about five miles south of Madison, probably one of first in Wisconsin. Picture taken by Andrew Dahl ca. 1876. Man at end of pond appears to be skimming weeds and algae. Board walk circles pond and drainage dam appears to be at right. Pond may be located at Nevin on Fish Hatchery Road.

"Coolidge Day" was celebrated in Wausau August 15, 1928 when President Calvin Coolidge came to address the state American Legion convention. Wearing top hat, hands resting on cane, he sits in back seat flanked by his son John and Mrs. Coolidge (barely visible). Louis Hall, a WWI veteran, drives Chrysler. Others are probably secret service.

There were many attempts in the early 1900s to convert sleighs to snowmobiles. The steam hauler traction engine used in the logging woods was fairly successful, but it took several decades before a practical snowmobile was developed for personal use. The one shown here was custom made by J. ("Jake") J. Healy of Antigo in 1909. It didn't work.

Opposite, upper, members of the Menominee tribe preparing for powwow in Woodland Bowl near Keshena, ca. 1960. Below, hostesses responsible for food and refreshments.

Small towns wanted to stage 4th of July celebrations not only because it was an exercise in patriotism, but also to prove to neighboring towns that this was an up-coming-place to be. Most small towns in early 20th Century had their own "cornet" band, and "Rosholt Cornet Band," seen leading parade of floats up Main Street, was no exception. "Insurance" on awning at right designates first State Bank of Rosholt building. Big building at corner of street is "dry goods" store of L.H. Mall. Rooms were rented upstairs to dentist and visiting doctor, and back rooms were rented to telephone "central." Photo taken about 1908.

Postcard picture of "Grand Rapids" band (now Wisconsin Rapids), ca. 1910. Bandstand in back was one of most common landmarks in Wisconsin in early decades of 20th Century. Villages as small as Rosholt had to have one. Here the local cornet band played on Saturday evenings to draw the farmers to town, and from this podium the LaFolletes, father and son, orated, and famous contraltos like Ernestine Schuman-Heink sang on Armistice day.

Rosholt Free Community Fair, incorporated in 1926, began with "Guernsey Picnic" in 1916. Postcard pictures seen here were taken in early 1920s. Local merchants have built booths or stalls. Wolding Hardware touts Oliver tractors and plows, and G.A. Gulickson has dealership for Ford Motor Company. Below: games of chance, one with ring to be tossed over top of cane, and one with balls to throw, (three for ten cents) to win a cigar or other prize. A feature of early fairs was an outside speaker or candidate for office, but main event was performance by Stevens Point band in "bandstand." There was no public address system and audience sat as close to center stage as possible.

An unseen hand has penciled this notation on the original of this picture: "M.E. Sunday School picnic, Mr. Brigham pastor." This was the Reverend Francis H. Brigham, pastor of the First Methodist Church, 306 Franklin Street, Wausau, Wisconsin. The picture was probably taken in the 1890s when bicyling was in its heyday. Groups like this often pedaled from one village to another on a Sunday outing. The Reverend Brigham may be seen in derby hat next to tree at right.

Deer hunters in early 1900s often occupied abandoned logging shanties such as this one probably in Marathon County. Taking two deer, buck or doe, was legal. No protective clothing was necessary. As a result more hunters were killed in season, in proportion to population, than at present. Deer are in pile here probably because hunters are waiting for wagon to take them and their trophies out of the woods.

Postcard, dated 1908, shows lady hunter in fringed buckskin jacket and four-point buck she shot, presumably in northern Wisconsin. There were no deer to hunt in central and southern Wisconsin in 1908. Pioneer settlers and Indians before them had decimated deer herd south of timber belt by 1900.

Party of deer hunters who shot four small does, one buck and a beaver (hanging on door). Instead of hunting shack, these hunters have rented a box car of the Green Bay & Western, installed stove and built door with hole for stove pipe. Coffee can stands on stove and lantern hangs above. Box car probably stood on old logging siding for duration of hunt. Some of the hunters seem to be carrying long-barreled 303 Savage. None wear protective clothing which was not required before late 1930s.

Protestants in America traditionally held outdoor "fests" and revivals in summer, highlighted by some outstanding speaker or missionary on home leave from China. This is probably a Norwegian-Lutheran congregation. Hardwood grove, with no pines around, suggests southern Wisconsin or Minnesota. A platform has been built where program is now in progress. Lady in white blouse and black hat leads two girls (at her left) in song, probably a hymn, while girl in braids plays organ. Local cornet band has already given one number at least and is expected to give another and what better place to store horn than in a tree? Note two young ladies at lower right, identical hats and blouses, probably twins.

Murphy Pledge

"With malice toward none, with charity for all."

I, the undersigned, do Pledge my word and honor,

GOD HELPING ME,

to abstain from All Intoxicating Liquors, as a beverage, and that I will, by all honorable means, encourage others to abstain.

Name *Miss Lottie Knapp*

Residence *Kilbourn, Wis.*

Date *July 20, 1899*

"Murphy Pledge" was part of national campaign to ban the sale of liquor in the United States which ended in triumph for anti-saloon forces with passage of the 18th Amendment in 1917, but repealed in 1933 by passage of the 21st Amendment to end Prohibition.

Crossing the high bridge at Wausau in an open sleigh, three bells tinkling on either shaft, Master Ben Alexander, teamster, shows his brother Collins and sister Ruth what the West Side is doing on this frosty day in winter about the year 1900.

An annual feature of village life in the early 1900s was a parade sponsored by the local booster club or advancement association. The one shown here was part of a "Farm Festival" held at Withee, Wisconsin, 1912. Grown-ups and children often dressed up in fancy custumes, or wore black face, as seen on boy at right. Boy in center wears false mustache, and parade marshall, on horseback, chews on big cigar.

Saloon keepers of Withee brought out this float in "Farmers Festival" held in 1912. Bunting is probably red, white and blue, and hand-picked orchestra sits in improvised lumber wagon to entertain crowd as parade moves past.

John Christiansen drove this gaily decorated car in the "Farmers Festival" parade at Withee.

Rice Lake parade, probably 4th of July, with horse drawn floats. Postcard picture, here enlarged, was taken about 1909 and manufactured in Germany.

Places of Business

Many ways of doing business a half a century ago have passed away or have been overtaken by methods forced upon us by new techniques, new products, new packaging, and new appetites. The explosion in technology is almost overwhelming and most of us wonder, in view of what has happened in the past fifty years as compared to the past thousand years, what on earth can we expect in the next 100? Perhaps nothing big; perhaps we have reached the zenith of creative activity. After all, a Boeing 727 can't get much bigger without redoing all our airport runways and control tower systems, and our cars can't get much wider, or faster, without enlarging our highways, and if we are forced into that, then there won't be much room left to raise potatoes or grow corn to fill our silos to feed our great herds of dairy cattle. Still, I wouldn't bet on it.

We can't get along without "wheels" either, but we can't seem to cope with them. People, even in small towns, are coming at you from every alley and intersection. Where are they coming from, or going to for that matter? Must be somewhere. And if you want to test the limit of your endurance in the driver's seat, try driving up, or down, the Ryan Expressway in Chicago at 3 p.m. But the locals get used to it. They can handle it.

Of course, we would not care to go back to the horse and buggy, or to the old places of business either, for on second thought, places of business a hundred years ago were not all that comfortable, and pool halls were not very clean. And certainly no dairyman is going to return to milking cows by hand and throw out the milking machine. Nor are potato farmers, despite the size and cost of their harvester, going back to digging spuds with a six-tine fork.

Still, we like to think that the "old days" were better, and that is one reason why the few pictures that have been assembled here are of interest. Take the one of Peter Lepak sawing ice on the Wisconsin River. He works with precision and he concentrates on the task at hand. He seems to like his work, but today it isn't necessary for anyone to stand on the cold ice and saw ice into blocks to be stored in an old ice house insulated with sawdust. We can make all the ice we need by mechanical means, a rebuff to nature which held a monopoly on the ice business for many years.

Still, there is something comforting about this picture of Mr. Lepak for there is a sense of unhurried time in what he is doing. Likewise, the picture of Louis Pfeifer's barber shop on Milwaukee's South Side. Customers are relaxed under a hot towel, not a hair blower, the way men have been relaxing since time out of hand and that goes back a long way.

In the picture of the lonely lighthouse at Racine's Wind Point we see another ghost from the past. The light to warn ships at sea goes on at night but there is no lighthouse keeper to light it. It goes on by itself and it stays on until it is shut off. It just doesn't seem right that after oil lamps and torches had been used for so many centuries to send out a ray of light to sea, that an even stronger light can be reflected by something most of us can't even define, namely, electricity. But just wait, some day there'll be a time for reckoning and we'll learn that removing the whale oil wasn't such a good idea, after all, because one of these days the juice isn't going to come on and then who will switch the light on at Wind Point? But fear not. By that time we probably won't need electrical juice to run our power plants, or even nuclear energy. Lighthouses and other places of business will be run on sources of energy yet undreamed of, probably extracts from sea weeds or maple sap!

One of the pictures in this chapter was taken inside a Gamble chain store. The owner, Fred Dahlen, like most franchise owners, has left no open space on floor, shelf or wall that he cannot find a product for, or an advertising poster to hang up. He has crammed more goods into less space than anyone can imagine. It used to be fun to ask him for something he did not have because he was certain that he just had it yesterday, but he'd get it for you next time the Gamble truck came around. At least he was there to wait on his customers. There was something cozy and personal about shopping here, and yet, after shopping at K-Mart, who can say if the Gamble stores have a chance for a come back or not? Our malls have changed a nation's shopping habits and while they are not as personal with customers, circumstantial evidence suggests that the shopping malls are here to stay.

BARREL STACKER IN OPERATION
AT JOS. SCHLITZ BREWING CO.
MARCH 14, 1937

Photo found in collection of pictures from archives of Wisconsin Bridge & Iron Company of Milwaukee, now defunct, which built and installed barrel stacker seen here.

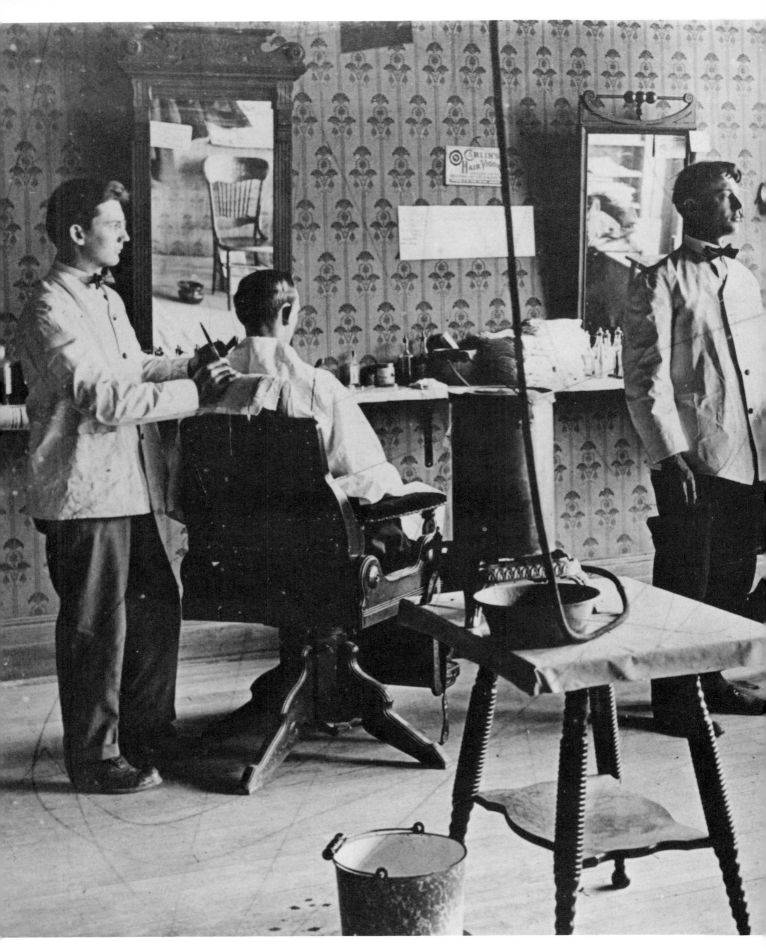

Louis Pfeifer (center) at his barber chair at 1259 National Avenue on Milwaukee's South Side, known in times past as "Silver City." At left, Louis' brother Albert, and at right, Mrs. Pfeifer, the former Oline Ingebretson of Alban township (Portage County). She acts as cashier and sells cigars. Electric cord from ceiling keeps water in container hot for shaving customers. Chair and spittoon are reflected in mirror behind Albert. Pfeifer was born in Stevens Point. He was also a veteran of the Spanish-American War, reputedly the youngest to enlist, at 15, in the army. He needed his mother's consent to an affidavit that said he was eighteen. When she refused, he threatened to take an ax and smash her sewing machine. She signed, and Louis went off to war, all the way to the Philippines before returning home, without a scratch. A few years after his discharge, he heard about a village being born called "Rosholt," located east of Stevens Point. He saw an opportunity to open the first barber shop and moved to the village in 1905. Here he met and fell in love with Oline Ingebretson and they were married and in 1907 they moved to Milwaukee.

Glass plate photo by William Zeit was taken in Medford, early 1900s, shows Brucker, Ludloff Company building located at northeast corner of Main and Division streets. Building later became First National Bank of Medford, and is presently occupied by Helen Lissner's resale shop. American flag flies from mast. Medford was largely settled by German emigrants from Prussia and other German states or principalities. On hill at right stands first court house of Taylor County.

In the 1850s a community of homes and a few stores grew around the mouth of the Little Plover River in Stevens Point called "Springville." A grist mill was built by John R. Mitchell and known for many years as "Mitchell's Mill." It was rebuilt under new owners in the 1880s but the mill burned and it was rebuilt again in 1899 by E.H. Rossier who operated it under the firm name of "Springville Milling." Lester Warner, 94, recalls bringing grain to be ground here. He referred to Rossier as "Ro-sher," a French pronounciation adopted locally. The mill dam washed out as this picture, taken in 1904 suggests, but dam was rebuilt and the mill continued to operate into the 1930s before it closed. The property passed to E.A. Oberweiser who tore the mill down and built a home on the same site. A private swimming pool today includes part of the old mill flume, or "race."

Peter Lepak cutting ice on Wisconsin River at Stevens Point for Olson Pure Ice Company, ca. 1940. Circular saws were also used to cut ice blocks, but hand-held saw was safest and most reliable. Ice blocks were shunted ashore and stored in big "ice houses" with blanket of sawdust on all sides. Electric refrigerators had largely replaced old fashioned ice box with pan underneath for drainage but Olson ice was still in business in 1947.

Park Hotel at corner of Main and Carroll streets in Madison as photogrpahed by Andrew Dahl, ca. 1875. Architecture is American Second Empire with a hybrid of Mansart roof with the Italianate style. It had no electricity or telephone. The wires running from pole at left are telegraph. Stage coach at corner met trains, and light wagon at right hauled heavy baggage and traveling salesmen sample trunks.

Wind Point Lighthouse at Racine as it looked when photographed by Oscar Lindquist about 1950. It was built in 1881 and lighthouse keepers through the years have included (NFN) Finch, Larry Easson, J. Sandel, Peter J. Peterson, Henry Bevry, Theodore Grosskoft, and Oscar Fransen. Automation began with the retirement of Fransen in March 1964. The residence below the light is now used as a public meeting place for Wind Point Village and the entire complex is maintained by the village under license from the United States Coast Guard.

Fred Dahlen (behind counter at right) got Gamble franchise to operate store in Rosholt in late 1930s and continued in business for next three decades.

When this picture was taken in early 1890s, these vehicles were referred to as "stages," but they were mail carriers on star routes in northwestern Wisconsin before the introduction of rural free delivery. Star routes only dropped mail at post offices. Driver in surrey at left is Ira Cable, later a railway man. Photo was taken at Clam Falls and house in background was probably a hotel where drivers spent night, and horses were rested and fed in barn (not visible) behind hotel.—Photo courtesy of Robert Cable.

Boardinghouse hotel at Phillips, Wisconsin, ca. 1890, catered to mill hands of John R. Davis Lumber Company, and to transient lumberjacks and businessmen. Hotel stood on north Main Street (Highway 13) on west side of road overlooking sawmill and yard. It was destroyed in great fire that swept through Phillips in 1893. Youth sits in cutter at left while his father holds bridle of horse to keep it quiet while picture being taken. Bar in hotel sold Milwaukee beer.

City of Medford, Wisconsin was carved out of wilderness after Wisconsin Central Rail Road built track through here in 1874 en route to Ashland. Above, first high school, with cupola for bell tower. Stumps in foreground wait for future work parties. Photo was taken by William Zeit, an immigrant from Austria, not long after he set up studio in city in 1880. School was located on northeast corner of 4th and Clark streets.

An anonymous photograph, using a glass plate for negative, took this picture of "The Senate Bar" at Sheply, a community lying northeast of Wittenberg in Shawano County. A sign behind the bar seems to read: "Never end beer," while picture behind bar is reflection from opposite wall. Saloon keeper takes pride in all the postcards people have sent him, one from Hawaii. At right is cooler, actually enlarged ice box.

Postcard picture (enlarged) of iron mine at North Freedom, ca. 1910.

A "horse dealer," more commonly called a "horse trader," has pitched his tent in a grove of trees outside of town where he can show his horses, most of which appear to be drivers. He carries a portable stove, coffee can and kettle. Rig at right carried tent, bedding and food supplies for move to next location. This is postcard picture, enlarged, taken by A.J. Kingsbury of Antigo, ca. 1910.

Members of the Portage County Board of Supervisors have picture taken in spring of 1956, the last board of supervisors to meet in the old Court House, built in early 1870s, and demolished in 1956 to make room for new court house on same site. Front row, l. to r., Craig Corbett, Harold Frost, Gilbert Kirby (chairman), Ernest Kluck, and Chester Kulas, clerk; 2nd row, left, Vincent Jurgella, William Petrusky, Henry Kurtzweil and Frank Steckel; 3rd row, left, Frank Beck, Nat Kinney, Joe Shroda, Tom Morgan and Joe Wojcik; 4th row, left, Arleigh Hetzel, Henry Doehr, Joe Glaza, Ted Burant and Paul Kitowski; 5th row, left, Ed Zurawski, Cliff Nebel, Ed Losinski, and A.P. Dobbe; 6th row, left, Harold Mehne, Charles Anderson, Milvern Jacklin, next not identified, and Henry Stinson; 7th row, left, Joe Hannon, Allen Barrows, Harold Anderson, Tom Guyant and Rowena Allen, county superintendent of schools; 8th row, left, Ray Pinkerton, county agent, Russell Krogwold, George Fletcher, Stanley Kirsling and Francis Mozuch; 9th row, left, John Burns, Henry Swenson, Perry Worden, highway commissioner, and Rube Lewis, county service officer. Absent from picture: John Jakusz, Martin Poliwada and Anton Palek.

A woodburner, 4-4-0, on Milwaukee & St. Paul Rail Road, approaches Middleton station in photo taken by Andrew Dahl, ca. 1875. Sign over door on building at left reads "Post Office."

Woodburner with diamond stack, probably Milwaukee Roader near Madison, waits for crew to clear track. Engine has small snow plow on pilot but not big enough to challenge big drift. Men with shovels and wheelbarrows did the job, and Andrew Dahl took picture, ca. 1875.

Sugar bush in Section 1, Town 25 North, Range 10 East. Photo by author taken in 1965.

Some Wisconsin Barnstormers

The word "barnstormer" comes from the stage. It originated in England where strolling players often moved from town to town, performing in sheds and barns in a "noisy style of ranting," according to the Oxford dictionary. They became known as barnstormers, and early airplane pilots, paid to thrill the crowds at county fairs with loops and wing-overs, also became known as barnstormers.

In 1983 a group of aviation enthusiasts, pilots and retired barnstormers got together in Appleton, Wisconsin to honor a pioneer Wisconsin pilot. They roasted him and told jokes, but they praised him mostly and sent him home with a fountain pen stand balanced by a gold-plated, single engine monoplane. The identification plate reads: "Elwyn West, Pioneer Aviator of the Fox River Valley."

For an old barnstormer who had to make out with a hay field for a runway when he began flying, it was an honor he enjoyed. He had been flying since he was tall enough to prop an engine.

But how does a farm boy from Lind Center in Waupaca County ever get started flying? He didn't have Lindbergh to inspire him. He had Ralph Conant, a barnstormer from Westfield who was making the county fairs in 1920, one of them the Waupaca County Fair at Weyauwega. And when he let down to pick up passengers, there was Elwyn West, a senior in High School, waiting to take his first ride, flying in a World War I surplus airplane called a "Standard", a biplane relative of the Curtiss J-N. West handed over the fare of $15 to Conant who pocketed the money and told him to climb into the front seat.

"And that fifteen bucks was the biggest thrill of my life," West later recalled. "After I finished High School, class of 1920 at Waupaca, all I could think of was flying I didn't want to farm, I didn't want to do anything but fly. Then I heard about a field in Chicago where they were giving instructions. Ashburn Field I think, and a couple of years after I got out of high school I took off for Chicago. When I got back, I began to save my money to buy my first Standard, a surplus plane which the government was selling for $150. I started right out, barnstorming, flying at the county fairs. But all I could take up in that old Standard was one passenger. The gas tank was lower than the carburetor and the gas had to be pumped up by hand. So I replaced the Standard's OX-5 with a Hisso,

and that gave me more horsepower, 150 in fact, and I could take up two passengers instead of one. That really put me in business.

"I had a small hangar on the home farm in Lind Center and I'd fly over to the George Whiting Airport north of Menasha, one of the first commercial airports in the state, right after the one the Larson Brothers built over there in Winchester. And I got to know all the guys who were flying and we'd brag and joke about our airplanes, all light aircraft . . . tell you that!

"In 1926 I began making the Rosholt Community Free Fair which was held every year over the Labor Day weekend, and I was there and had a great time. I remember there was a small block house, sort of, at the end of my run and I always had to be careful not to hit it with my landing gear. It wasn't over six feet high but it was made of concrete blocks, one time used for storing dynamite. I kept going back to Rosholt for many years. I remember the man I made the arrangements with was Peterson, Lester Peterson. And I remember one year I sent another pilot with one of my airplanes to Rosholt while I went up to the fair at Escanaba. The new pilot I sent to Rosholt made one run and nearly flipped over in a cross wind and he refused to fly any more. But I respected his judgment. I still had my airplane. Next year, I couldn't make Rosholt either and a barnstormer from Winona, Max Conrad, came up and wouldn't you know, he clipped that blockhouse and flipped over. He wasn't hurt much but one of his passengers broke an arm. His ship was washed out."

When asked what type of aircraft he was flying on his first visit to Rosholt, Mr. West said: "I was flying the old Canadian Curtiss, the 'Canuck' we called it, a first cousin of the Jennie."

Mr. West was one of the first pilots to fly off George Whiting Airport when a hangar was built from an old barn north of Menasha on what was then called Air Port Road. Construction of the airport was encouraged by Paper Maker George

Whiting and other business leaders in the Fox River Valley. In 1935, with the help of the Works Project Administration (WPA) the airport was moved east of Ballard Road where it became known as the Outagamie County Airport.

"Of course, I'd fly anywhere but I wasn't doing any trick stuff or flying circus," Mr. West insisted. "Strictly business with me. After World War II began, I was too old for the Air Corps but I worked for more than a year, instructing cadets at the county airport, and then I heard about a deal up in Ely, Minnesota, way up there in the lake country next to the Canadian border. There were resorts on the lakes and the fishing was good, but the most practical way to get into these resorts was on floats. So I flew up there in the spring of 1943 and built a small hangar on Lake Shagawa, on the north side of Ely, and I began to carry passengers and supplies into the resort country, using my floats to land on the lakes."

"He wasn't flying his Canuck any more. "Oh, Lord no, but almost anything else I could get my hands on. This was war time and we had to have a good excuse to fly and burn gas. My first plane up there was a Canadian Norseman, a ten-place job. Then I got two Waco cabins, five place, and I had two Piper J-3s on floats, and another Piper, a PA-12, three place, on wheels, and a Curtiss Robin, a four place amphibian. The last one I got was a Sebie built by Republic, a four place amphibian."

He wasn't flying this air fleet by himself. "Oh, no, no. I hired old barnstormers to help me and I also found a good mechanic to maintain my aircraft, and then one day the federal aviation people heard about me and they flew in and told me I didn't have enough mechanics to provide good maintenance and that was the beginning of my troubles with the feds."

"How so? Well I'll tell you, the feds wanted to enlarge Superior National Forest which runs along the Canadian border and the government was buying up as many resorts as it could. Make this a wild life refuge, but the resort owners were mad as hell. On July 3, 1953 I flew my last airplane back to Waupaca County, and got started with a game farm, raising buffalo, elk and deer."

Elwin West now lives in retirement near the farm where he was born in Lind Center. He was not only a pioneer aviator to Wisconsin but also one of the best. He never lost an airplane; he never hurt anyone seriously, and he never hurt himself except for a scratch on the chin. He was a pilot who did his homework and kept his mind on his fuel gauge and on his navigation, and learned never to challenge an old dynamite house in Rosholt.

Elwyn West in his first airplane, a Canadian Curtiss JN-4 which was purchased from government surplus and assembled on family farm in Lind Center in 1922. In front seat is Luther West, a younger brother, later to lose his life in a crash in Minnesota.

Elwyn West in front of Standard with OX-5 90 HP engine. Picture taken on family farm in Lind Center, Waupaca County.

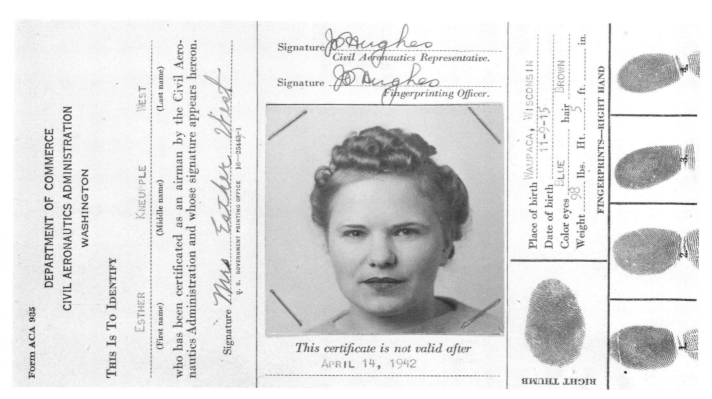

Esther West, wife of Elwyn West, was one of first licensed women pilots in Wisconsin.

Aerial view of Whiting Airport, ca. 1929. Stinson at left. Other aircraft include two Waco-10s, a Swallow and a Travel Air.

Ford tri-motor at Whiting Airport, ca. 1932. Elwyn West was first manager of airport before field was abandoned and new facility built on Ballard Road called Outagamie County Airport.

Aerial view of hangar (left) at George Whiting Air Port on one-time Whiteman farm north of Menasha.

Ford tri-motor at Whiting airport.

George Whiting Airport, ca. 1930 with Tri-motored Stinson at left. Second from left probably Travel Air, next a Waco-10, and last on right probably Waco-9.

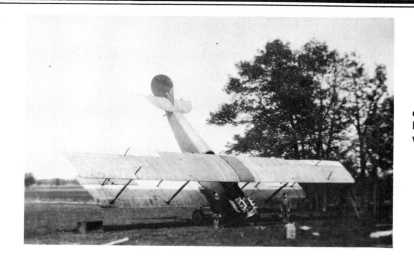

This Canadian Curtiss has been up-ended for engine work by Elwyn West on the family farm in Lind Center. Light airframe made this easy. Picture was taken in early 1920s.

A Standard with OX-5 engine at Outagamie County Airport, ca. 1939.

A Stinson at Outagamie County Airport, ca. 1939.

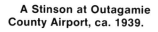

THE LARSON BROTHERS

On September 29, 1985, Leonard and Viola Larson dedicated an unusual historical marker. It stands on the north side of Highway 150 east of Winchester in Winnebago County. The bronze plaque, embedded in field stone, also stands at the south end of a hayfield that was once a runway used by the Larson family of aviation pioneers. On the north end of the runway stands a hangar, probably the oldest in Wisconsin. It was built by the four Larson Brothers, Roy, Clarence, Newell and Leonard in 1923-24.

In an interview with Roy Larson in 1985 there was time for remembering, for Leonard, now the only surviving brother, has much to remember about old airplanes and engines.

Barnstorming began in Wisconsin about 1920, shortly after the federal government began to dispose of World War I surplus airplanes, engines, and parts. An engine could be bought on a bid for $100 and an air frame for about the same, freight on board not included.

Said Mr. Larson: "My brother Roy started flying in 1922. He learned to fly at Ashburn field on the south side of Chicago. A fellow named Ralph Diggings was his first instructor and he was using a Jenney, actually a Curtiss Canuck made in Canada. Roy borrowed money to buy his first air frame and the first thing he did was to install an OX-5 engine. We kept it in the haybarn at first but then the next year we got to work on a hangar. That airplane was a Standard and Elwyn West had a Canuck which he kept in our hangar too."

In 1926 Roy Larson got the franchise for the Waco-9 and sold four, one to West and one to Johnny Wood from Wausau, and one to Howard Morey from McFarland, and one to Gene Shanks from Minneapolis. "Shanks had the world record," Mr. Larson said, "for continuous rolls, but Speed Holman had the record for loops. Anyway, Roy taught me to fly and we went barnstorming all over the state until Roy got killed in Appleton, in 1929, while instructing a student there. The student must have blacked out or something because he was dead on impact but Roy lived three days. Before that he had also got hold of a Waco-10. Same engine in both airplanes. The Waco-10 weighed about 1300 pounds. The Waco-9 was lighter. The 10 flew good but it wasn't as good for barnstorming. The 9 had more wing area and was better on take-off."

Larson Brothers hanger at Winchester, ca. 1926. At left, a Waco-9; in center a Standard; and at right, a Waco-10.

"Do I remember any other barnstormers? I remember one from Stanley, Emmett Kyle, and there was Slim Peterson from Owen-Withee. He got hold of a Laird from Charlie Holman in Minneapolis, the one they called 'Speed Holman.' But it was in pretty bad shape, and I remember a guy they called James Blue. Seems to me he got a Stinson tri-motor from someone in Alaska. I mentioned the Laird. What I meant was the Laird Solution and it was in one of them that John Page got killed in Chicago. I talked to Mr. Laird one time in Chicago at the Curtiss-Wright plant there. He put lots of weight into that airplane, a real popular plane with the barnstormers."

"Before Roy died, we were all over the state. Must have landed on a 100 fields and newly-built airports, but most of the time we were flying off race tracks like the one at the Portage County Fair in Stevens Point. In those days we were getting five bucks a passenger. Roy once took up an old Civil War veteran who was so pleased to be flying that he gave him a five dollar gold piece. But, by 1925, we had to cut the price of a ticket to $2.50 and business picked up. I already had 600 hours and Roy more than 2000. Al Gruanke from Appleton had 1000 hours. Roy often landed at Whitman Airport in Oshkosh and also at Stilson's on the south side off Highway 45. I remember in 1931 I was invited by the Menomonee Indians to come to Kenosha where I landed on a town road. I took passengers up over the Wolf River and one of them said he was more than pleased because he had spotted some trout holes he had never seen before.''

In 1925 the federal aviation bureau advised all barnstormers and commercial pilots that they would have until 1928 to be certified for a federal license. O.W. Young was the first aviation inspector in central Wisconsin. In 1931 the regulations were changed and pilots had to have so many hours in the air every year or lose their license. ''That meant,'' said Mr. Larson, ''that we had to keep flying or be grounded. We were issued a so-called transport license, according to weight classification of our aircraft, 600 pounds I think, and if you went into heavier planes, or transports, you had to have a different license.''

After Roy Larson died, Leonard continued to barnstorm but when the Depression ''come along I had to cut the price of a ride to $1 but I continued to barnstorm but it was not the same with Roy gone. He taught me everything I knew about flying and about engines. After we got into World War II, I was too old for the Air Corps, but I was hired as a civilian instructor in the glider program which had been set up at Antigo. There was, at this time, I think, only two other schools for gliders. Andrew Anderson had a flying school in Antigo which was converted to a glider school. Howard Morey was in charge, I believe, at Janesville.''

Asked what the glider program consists of, Mr. Larson replied: ''We had no gliders to train with. All we had was the Cub. We took the future glider pilots up, then turned back to the field to shoot dead stick. This went on all day. We didn't even have a self starter on the Cub and it had to be propped every time we took off. But to save time for instructors who would have had to get out of the cockpit every time they landed, there were several guys on motorcycles who kept moving around the field and when I raised my hand they would race over to my airplane and give the prop a twist.''

''What was I making? I was making $225 a month but, since I was a civilian, I had to board myself and find my own lodging. The other civilian instructors were in the same boat. After finishing at Antigo, I was asked to go to Missouri, and from then on through the rest of the war, I served as a mechanic on aircraft at different fields, Eau Claire, Milwaukee and Chicago. I remember Sig Wilson from Marquette, Michigan. He was in Milwaukee in charge of 100-hour periodics. Mostly Liscombe Continental engines. Kenneth Crawford from Berlin was there too.''

Marker dedicated September 29, 1985 off Highway 150 east of Winchester, Winnebago County.

Asked what was the last airplane he flew, Mr. Larson said it was a Waco he bought after WWII, not for barnstorming, but because it was an airplane and because it seemed lonesome around the old hangar without one. But finally that had to go too. No more flying. Now there are no airplanes on ''Larson Field,'' only memories. Mr. Paul Poberezny, founder of the Experimental Aircraft Association, was on hand at the marker dedication to help preserve some of these memories.

EMMETT A. KYLE

Emmett Kyle learned to fly at the Lambert Flying School in St. Louis in the late 1920s and, as a commercial pilot, he was required to keep a log, that is, a record of every flight he made and how many hours, or minutes, he spent in the American Air Space.

His home was in Stanley, but on the front page of Log Book #2, begun May 29, 1930, he gives his business address as the Richfield Road Airport at Marshfield.

Mr. Kyle's first logbook is unavailable but his widow, Anne, now living in retirement in Stanley, had preserved his second book which runs from May 20, 1930 to September 16, 1934. In the period from May 29, 1930 to May 11, 1931 he was flying his own Travel Air, the "Silver Hare," and on June 2, 1931 he began to fly a Waco which was owned by Dr. J.S. Hess Jr. of Mauston. Whether flying the Travel Air or the Waco, he often picked up passengers or went barnstorming at local fairs and picnics.

The Travel Air, #C-6993, was powered by the OX-5 and the Waco by the J-5 Wright, the same used by Lindbergh in his "Spirit of St. Louis." Of the two, the OX-5 was, historically, the most famous.

The first OX-5 was built by Glenn Curtiss in 1912 and continued in production until 1918, ending up as the main engine for the JN4, better known as the "Jenny" in the U.S. and as the "Canuck" in Canada. Not less than 12,000 or more than 13,000 were built. After World War I the federal government released thousands from surplus for $50 each, F.O.B.

The Ox-5 that Emmett Kyle used was probably an eight cylinder V-type (90 degree), water cooled engine capable of 90 H.P. at 1400 RPM, and swung a prop that was more than eight feet in diameter. Since 1955, an elite club has grown, worldwide, of members who once flew or worked on the OX-5, with "wings" in most of the fifty states.

Meanwhile, in 1930, Pilot Kyle touched down in his Travel Air at Marshfield, Wisconsin Rapids, Chippewa Falls, Jump River, Owen, Sparta, Mineral Point, Spring Green, Richland Center, Mauston, Merrill, Phillips, Park Falls, Platteville and several towns in Iowa. In 1931 he touched down at Des Moines, Cedar Rapids and Arndale, Iowa, as well as on fields in Wisconsin such as Camp Douglas, Brookfield, Loyal, Portage, Eau Claire and Menomonee.

Emmett Kyle's Travel Air (The "Silver Hare") ca. 1930.

In October 1931 he flew Dr. Hess's Waco from Mauston to Binghamton, New York, a nine hour flight, and from Binghamton to Bethany, Connecticut, and Bethany to Camden, New Jersey and on to Roosevelt Field, Long Island. He then turned around and flew back, the last leg the longest from Hazelton, Pennsylvania to Mauston in 10:35 hours. After refueling at Mauston on October 26, he returned to Stanley the following day in one hour and ten minutes.

Flying the Waco for Dr. Hess in 1932, Pilot Kyle often flew from Mauston to Chicago, or to Boyd, Tomah, to Milwaukee and to Ashland. He often gave instructions to students in the Waco, and on occasion did stalls, wing overs and vertical banks and "night flying."

On September 25, 1932, he took his Waco on an altitude flight when he climed to 17,300 feet, which was about the limit he could go without oxygen.

On May 13, 1933, although he was still flying Dr. Hess' Waco, he flew a "New Standard" on a local flight, and again on May 14 when he was apparently giving instructions in the New Standard. He continued for several days giving instructions in the New Standards and then returned to the cockpit of the Waco and flew from Manitowoc to Denmark but he fails to say how he got to Manitowoc.

On May 28, 1930 he made a test hop at Wisconsin Rapids in a H.R. 21 Fairchild. On May 23 1933 he made a test hop in a Robin NC922K with Challenger engine. On June 26, 1934 he made a test hop at Manitowoc in a Swallow NC5345 with OX-5 engine, but he was aloft only ten minutes.

On August 10, 1933 Pilot Kyle says he made a local flight at Mauston in a Ford NC7685 with 3-J-5 engine, in other words a tri-motor, but he fails to explain when he was checked out in three-engine aircraft. But, on August 22, same year, he was up in another Ford C-7583 for ten minutes with "passengers," field uncertain.

His log mentions, at different times, "practice maneuvers," or "flight with contact," or "test flight and instruction" (in the Waco), "safety piloting with student," or "wing overs" and practice "blind flying in clouds."

On May 22, 1933 he made a test hop in a Robin, NC922K with Challenger engine. On June 26, 1934 he made a test hop at Manitowoc in a Swallow, NC5345, with OX-5 engine, but he was in the air only ten minutes.

Pilot Kyle gained newspaper coverage in 1933 in Juneau County. Bank robbers were on the loose and the county sheriff, having had a tip that the robbers were hiding in the woods around Castle Rock, asked Kyle to make an aerial search and he found them!

On two occasions in 1932, Kyle took part in air races, the first at Wisconsin Rapids on August 13, and the second on August 20 at Waupaca, but these races were short and fast, only ten minutes air time. After 1934, Kyle spent several years in aviation mechanics and finally bought a farm near Stanley where he lived until retirement. He died in 1985 and is buried at St. Mary's Cemetery in Stanley.

Early in July 1933, the State Bank of New Lisbon was held up by two robbers who escaped into nearby woods around Castle Rock in Juneau County. Sheriff Morgan Rider (left) asked Emmett Kyle (in goggles) to make a reconnaisance and he spotted them from the air and landed on a nearby hay field to tell the sheriff's posse where the fugitives were. This picture was taken at Mauston on July 11, 1933 shortly after the capture. The Waco, probably an F, was owned by Dr. J.S. Hess Jr. of Mauston. Man in center and youth in cockpit are not identified.

FORM AB-72-A

UNITED STATES OF AMERICA
DEPARTMENT OF COMMERCE
AERONAUTICS BRANCH

OFFICIAL NO.

10843

MECHANIC'S LICENSE

This Certifies, That Emmett A. Kyle

whose signature and photograph accompany this license,
is a licensed

Airplane & Engine MECHANIC

of civil aircraft of the United States of America.

Unless sooner suspended or revoked this license expires

March 15, 1936

U. S. GOVERNMENT PRINTING OFFICE: 1925   11—9671 **Assistant** Director of Aeronautics.

Below: First two pages from the log of Emmett Kyle, his second log book, begun May 7, 1930.

DATE OF FLIGHT	AIRCRAFT AND ENGINE USED ON THESE FLIGHTS			DURATION OF FLIGHT		STATE POINTS BETWEEN WHICH FLIG... STATE NATURE OF SUCH FLIGHTS. OCCURS, MAKE NOTATION UNDER RE... COMMERCE REGULATIONS.	
				HRS.	MIN.		
	MAKE OR TYPE OF AIRCRAFT	IDENTIFICATION OR LICENSE NO.	MAKE OR TYPE OF ENGINE	BROUGHT FORWARD		FROM	TO
				2 0			
Apr 28 30	Travel air	C-6093	OX5	1	40	Wise	Chiyenn...
May 7th 30	Travel air	C-6093	OX5		25	Stanley	Thompson...
May 10-30	Travel air	C6093	OX5	1	30	Stanley	Thompson...
May 15th 30	Travel...			1	05	Stanley to	Long River
May ...	Travel air	...6093	OX5	1	...	...	...
May 8...	Travel air	C6093	OX5		45	...	...
May 11th	Travel air	C 6093	OX5		20	...	...
May 31st	Travel air	C6093	OX5	1	...	Stanley	Minot...
...	...	...09...	...		...	...	...
...	...	...	...	1	40	...	...
...	...	...	...		...	...	...
May 28th	N.R.81	NC.363... Miner			15	...	...
					5 0		

TOTAL TIME TO BE CARRIED FORWARD

I CERTIFY THE ABOVE FLIGHTS WERE

ATTESTED BY_____

120

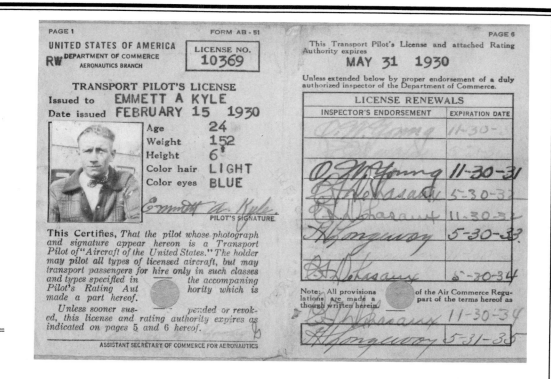

FORM AB - 51 PAGE 6

UNITED STATES OF AMERICA
RW DEPARTMENT OF COMMERCE
AERONAUTICS BRANCH

LICENSE NO.
10369

This Transport Pilot's License and attached Rating
Authority expires
MAY 31 1930

Unless extended below by proper endorsement of a duly
authorized inspector of the Department of Commerce.

TRANSPORT PILOT'S LICENSE
Issued to EMMETT A KYLE
Date issued FEBRUARY 15 1930

Age 24
Weight 152
Height 6'
Color hair LIGHT
Color eyes BLUE

PILOT'S SIGNATURE

This Certifies, *That the pilot whose photograph
and signature appear hereon is a Transport
Pilot of "Aircraft of the United States." The holder
may pilot all types of licensed aircraft, but may
transport passengers for hire only in such classes
and types specified in the accompanying
Pilot's Rating Authority which is
made a part hereof.*
*Unless sooner suspended or revoked,
this license and rating authority expires as
indicated on pages 5 and 6 hereof.*

ASSISTANT SECRETARY OF COMMERCE FOR AERONAUTICS

LICENSE RENEWALS	
INSPECTOR'S ENDORSEMENT	EXPIRATION DATE
	11-30-
O. M. Young	11-30-31
	5-30-32
	11-30-32
	5-30-33
	5-30-34
	11-30-34
	5-31-35

Note: All provisions of the Air Commerce Regulations are made a part of the terms hereof as
though written herein.

UNITED STATES OF AMERICA
DEPARTMENT OF COMMERCE
AERONAUTICS BRANCH

MECHANIC'S IDENTIFICATION CARD

This Identification Card, *issued on the*
23rd *day of* Sept. *, 19*31, *accompanies*
Mechanic's License No. 10843
DESCRIPTION OF HOLDER
Age 25
Weight 162 Color hair Light
Height 6' Color eyes Blue
De Lasaux

FORM AB-72

Mechanic's Signature.

ROLAND ZIEGLER

When you listen to Roland Ziegler tell about his days as a barnstorming parachute jumper it sounds like something straight out of Disneyland. As a junior in Appleton High School, in 1928, at age sixteen, he was jumping and getting paid for it.

Gottlieb Ziegler, Roland's father, was a founder and first president of Aid Association for Lutherans. But he had no idea he had a son who was defying the laws of gravity and the insurance business with thoughts of airplanes and parachute jumping at a time when neither was a very good risk.

But the boy spent his spare time out at the old George Whiting Airport listening to pilots like Elwyn West brag about their World War I surplus aircraft like the Standard with OX-5 engine. After Lindbergh flew the Atlantic in May 1927, Roland was convinced that the future was in the air, not on the ground.

But to become a pilot like Charles Lindbergh one had to learn to fly an airplane. The short-cut into the air was to become a parachute jumper and jump from someone else's airplane.

From an advertisement, Roland learned that a chute would cost $290. But where to get the money? He did not dare to ask his parents. Instead he wrote to Esther, a sister living in Detroit and asked to borrow the money from her. Also, no mention of this to his parents or the deal was off. She agreed.

A money order went off to the Irving Parachute Company in Buffalo, New York, and a few days later, Roland was advised he had a box at the post office. But where could he hide it? The Zieglers lived on East Pacific Street, two houses down from Alex Ogilvie, and their son Douglas, several years younger than Roland, idolized Roland because he was always talking about airplanes.

Douglas Ogilvie was sworn to secrecy and in this clandestine operation he agreed to hide the parachute in his attic. And here the two conspirators opened the box. There was the chute, neatly packed, waiting for someone who had the nerve to use it.

"So who taught you how to jump?" I asked.

"No one. A book of instruction came with the chute and I studied that backwards and forwards. Heck, it wasn't much to it. Just jump out and pull the string."

I was getting goose pimples listening to this man, now in his mid-seventies, and I said, "But

Roland Ziegler, 17, holds unpacked parachute, George A. Whiting Airport, 1929.

who taught you to pack the chute?" and he said, "No one. It was all there in that book."

"You're kidding," I said, "and if you didn't pack it right, then what?"

"Then you go back and get a new one," and he laughed as the memories came back, filling him with pleasure. "I made my first jump with Elwyn West. He was managing the airport, the Whiting out there on Air Port Road north of Menasha, and he agreed to take me up, over some field, when no one was looking, and up I flew and down I went, just like that. No trouble at all. And Elwyn hired me to jump at the county fairs where he was barnstorming. He would advertise that someone was going to jump and he delayed my jump as long as he could. That way more people came to spend money to ride in his airplane. I got $20 a jump."

"How high did you jump from?"

"About 1500 feet."

"And you had no spare chute?"

"No. But I did get a bigger chute, a 28-foot canopy and that made a big difference, a back pack too, not a seat pack. I never broke a bone but one time I nearly went into the brink at Neenah pond. I landed on top of a house. Next thing I knew, some people were carrying me downstairs. Except for some bad bruises, I was okay."

Roland Ziegler attended Lawrence College and was graduated in 1935. At this time he borrowed $1100 from his father, $700 of it for an airplane, and $400 to learn to fly. He got his private license which allowed him to fly and he went into busi-

ness for the Filmite Oil Company as a salesman, and attracted customers by advertising free rides with the purchase of five quarts of motor oil.

In World War II he went into the Army Air Corps but was turned down for flight training because of weak eyes. He now lives in retirement in California.

Ziegler testing canopy of new chute, a 28-footer.

Two Waco 10's used by Ziegler in promoting and delivering Filmite motor oil, with oil can logo on tail section and private pilot registration number.

Lincoln Beachey, pioneer stunt man and daredevil pilot, flew exhibition flights over Langlade County Fair grounds in this Curtiss pusher in 1912. He was engaged to come to Antigo by David Stewart, president of the fair association, for a fee probably of a thousand dollars. Three years later he lost a wing over San Francisco Bay and plunged to his death.

John G. Kaminski and his Curtiss pusher (the "Sweeetheart") probably a model D in photo taken in 1913 at the Silver Lake Aviation School at Cuyahoga Falls, Ohio. Kaminski, born in Milwaukee, 1893, was 18 years old when he learned to fly at the Glenn Curtiss School of Aviation located at North Island in San Diego, California. After completing a ten-week course of instruction, he was issued license #121 by the Aero Club of America under the auspices of the Federation Aeronautique Internationale, Paris, France. With war in Europe already under way, Kaminski, in 1916, joined a cadre of aviators under the Signal Corps of the U.S. Army as a flight instructor. After America's entry in the war in April 1917, he was prepared to go overseas when his orders were changed to proceed to the Canal Zone where he later flew the first air mail across the Isthmus of Panama. Here an accident changed his life. He was standing by while an attendant was about to fill his gas tank when the hose, carelessly handled by the attendant, splashed gas in Kaminski's eyes. He managed to continue to fly with special glasses and goggles but on his discharge from the army, he was advised to give up flying. He later worked in the postal department at Milwaukee, and died in February 1960. The Curtiss shown here was restored by Dale Crites and donated to the EAA Museum at Oshkosh.

124

Richard Ira Bong, born in Poplar, Wisconsin, became top all-time American fighter ace in World War II, scoring forty "victories" while flying with P-38 squadrons in Southwest Pacific. He was decorated with the Medal of Honor by General MacArthur in 1944. In summer of 1945, still attached to U.S. Air Force, he was on special duty as a test pilot for Lockheed when he was killed in a crash in California on August 6. He is buried in Poplar. A P-38 in his markings is mounted on a pylon located off Highway 2. On July 26, 1986 he was inducted into the National Aviation Hall of Fame at Dayton, Ohio. In picture at right he is shown in a P-38, probably an L, after returning from the Pacific.— U.S. Air Force photo, courtesy Mike O'Connor.

Larson Brothers airport at Winchester, early 1920s. At left is Roy Larson's Standard and at right, Elwyn West's. West has painted Army Air Corps colors on tail section. Note stripe.

Oscar Chapin of Birnamwood moved to Chippewa Falls where he barnstormed and took up passengers in the 1930s. He was killed in a crash, together with two passengers, in 1935, and he is buried at Forest Hill Cemetery in Chippewa Falls where this headstone appears with biplane.

John Schwister of Wausau, one of first pilots in the Wisconsin air space, is shown here in homemade Curtiss pusher, ready for takeoff, August 6, 1911. He wears football headgear and leather puttees in case of accident. He will need both. He was trying to come down on the local golf course, landed long and crashed, but walked away from it. After the U.S. went to war in 1917, he was killed while instructing air cadets.

Elwyn and Esther West at Ely, Minnesota under wing of J-3 Piper Cub. Timber wolf brought bounty of $35 in 1944. Hunters spotted game from air and landed on nearby ice with skis and pursued game on foot.

Postcard picture, enlarged, of balloon resting on ground at Withee, probably during "Farmer's Festival" days in summer of 1912. Balloon landed in present city park.

Reidar Olson built his own type pusher in Norway in 1913. In 1922 he emigrated to Merrill, Wisconsin where he followed his interest in aviation. In 1923 he moved to Tomahawk where he built a biplane dubbed "OSACO 6" with 17 HP engine, which he later cracked up. He moved to Chippewa Falls in 1928 where this monoplane, the "Olson Scout" was made, using a Szekely 30 HP engine. The logo on the fuselage reads "Chippewa Aircraft Corporation." Two of the "Scouts" were built and kits were assembled for self-built aircraft. More than twenty kits were sold before Depression and the end of the company.

COUNTY I

AT STANLEY, WIS.

ʼHURS., FRIDAY, SEPT. 1

The World's Greatest Aviator

RALPH E. McMILLAN

Two Flights Daily
from the
Fair Grounds
Rain or Shine in a
Gentle Wind or a
Tornado

See the
Wonderful Spiral Glide
from the
Clouds to Earth
See the
Great War Biplane

The famous Curtiss Biplane used in these flights is the same model of a machine as is now being used by the French and Germans in the great war.

The machine will be on exhibition every day at the Fair Grounds

---

All children under 16 free | **FRIDAY IS CHILDREN'S DAY** | All children under 16 free

---

FREE   ***EVERY NIGHT***   **FREE**
IN THE CITY
Grand Band Concert and Vaudeville Acts

Grand Parade Before the Grand Stand of Prize Stock Friday at 2 p. m.

MERRY - GO - ROUND
Shooting Galleries
Side Shows

Pit Shows, Baby Racks, Riding Devices, Novelty Wheels

$1,

f

Free

The L

Novelty tight w
on the wire as i
chairs, dancing,
doing the sensa
a barrel on the

Free Eve

Logging and Lumbering

At the close of the 19th Century, logging in the woods and sawing logs into lumber at the mills was the leading industry of Wisconsin. In fact, in 1894, Wisconsin led all other states in the production of lumber, railway ties and other forest products. Some early observers, interviewed in the press, were of the opinion that there was an inexhaustible supply of timber in Wisconsin. It would grow as fast as it could be cut.

But within twenty-five years after these optimistic predictions, man, the pigmy against the pines, was looking across vast stretches of cut-over land and slashings where the pine had once stood. What makes this even more remarkable is that most of these trees were hacked down by teams of choppers, one man swinging an ax from the left, one from the right, until the tree was falled. (Woodsmen never "fell" a tree!)

It was not until the beginning of the 1890s that the crosscut saw began to replace the ax, and then two men with a crosscut could fall nearly twice as many trees in one day as two men with axes.

Although most of the virgin pine is gone, much of it has already been replaced by second growth which stands 75 to 100 feet high, and there is probably more pine, if not red pine, growing in Wisconsin today than there was a century ago largely through replanting by paper makers, farmers, and tree growers on forest crop programs.

The pioneer period of lumbering saw much waste in the processing of logs into lumber at the sawmill. Early mills used a reciprocating saw blade, suspended vertically over the log, often called the "up and down" saw, which sawed through a log leaving half an inch kerf. They were replaced by circular saws, much thinner, and finally by band saws even thinner which produced more lumber and less sawdust. But early lumbermen often had to leave logs they had cut in winter to rot in the woods because of an early spring when the snow melted prematurely and it became impossible for a team of horses with sleighs to bring logs out.

In the decades between 1840 and 1870 in Wisconsin, there was no way to get lumber to the big markets on the Mississippi except by building the lumber into cribs and floating the cribs down the Wisconsin, the Chippewa or St. Croix rivers. Often these cribs ran into sandbars and became bogged down; other times the cribs hit a dam or a rock and broke up, strewing lumber all over the river and into the bayous and bogs and were left there because it did not pay to delay the other cribs and crews.

Before 1900, most logs cut in the forest had to be floated down rivers too, such as on the Chippewa and on the Wolf. These logs were floated to sawmills in Chippewa Falls, or to Shawano on the Wolf and to mills in Fond du Lac and Oshkosh. Always there was risk and all too often there were losses because the river rose over night, or fell below expectations, and whenever nature played hard-ball with the log drivers, there were losses and there was waste in logs left stranded or stolen by local pirates along the course of the river.

Records of early sawmill owners show that the big ones with capital to back them could survive a fire, or destruction of a mill, but small operators often went bankrupt after a fire, unable to pay the high insurance rates demanded for these highly flamable structures. Water barrels were required by insurance companies on the ridge board of the sawmills, but it would be difficult to find anyone who ever saw or heard of any water barrel that was used to put out a fire.

After the Iron Horses moved into the woods to speed up logging operations, sparks, despite arresters, often floated into the air and settled in the timber to start fires. Think of the fires at Peshtigo in 1871 and at Phillips in 1893. Once the fires got started, there seemed to be no way of stopping them because the land was dry after a long period without rain. We would like to blame the old logging trains for starting fires, but we are brought up short when we think of the thousands of acres of timberland being destroyed every year today, often by careless campers, but more often by the whims of nature, high winds and lightning.

The pine forests of Wisconsin were harvested because they were needed and they served the living. The lumber products were needed for building homes and barns on the Western prairies where there was no timber, while the hemlock, cedar and tamarack were needed for cross-ties on the road beds of the railroads opening up the west to commerce and to settlement. In the following pages are highlights of this great era of logging and lumbering in Wisconsin.

Basic work crew in logging woods in 1890s included ox teamster (left) who skidded logs out of woods to logging road; man with canthook is swamper who also used axe to trim fallen tree of limbs and to clear away brush impeding removal of log. Two at right are sawyers, both balancing crosscut saws on shoulders, the one at right also holding measuring stick, probably eight feet long. Two lengths of stick would be 16 feet, the most common length used for logs in this period. In this camp, at least, sawyers have replaced choppers to fall trees. Vehicle in right background is a box mounted on sleigh runners which C.J. Monroe "traveling photographer" used to carry his photographic equipment, glass plates and chemicals in visits to camps. Man in center may be more than twenty years old but his comrades are younger. One at right has had brush with a limb. Note patch over eye. Photo taken near Black River Falls.

These two pictures show the most common methods of decking logs. In picture above, the logs are being rolled up and over by a long decking chain hitched to the team at lower left on "cross-haul" technique. In photo below a portable jammer, commonly called a "woods jammer," is being used to deck the logs. A long cable ran from the team to a top block on top of long gin pole, and thence down to the ground where a log was hooked to the cable with pup-hooks and raised in the air by the team of horses pulling on block and tackle. Photo above shows men on deck, called "top loaders," who decide where each log should be dropped. Crews were employed by Louis Jacobson and Lawrence Peterson who had camp near Crandon in 1916-17. James Parfitt took the pictures, here slightly enlarged, for postcard sales.

Brooks & Ross Lumber Company of Schofield was logging in Langlade County in early 1900s. Landing shown here was near Kempster, north of Antigo, and logs were hauled on these wide-bunked sleighs to Deerbrook where they were dumped into Eau Claire River for drive to big sawmill in Schofield. Second load in picture is not quite filled up, and top loaders are using cross-haul technique to roll logs to top of load. Note two skid poles on which logs are rolled upward. Cross-haul team which pulled logs up is hidden at left. These loads represent about as much as two horses could pull on snow-covered roads not iced by tankers.

Both these pictures of over-sized loads of logs are part of woods mythology. Logs were decked expressly for benefit of cameraman who got as many of crew on picture as possible with view to future sales. These big loads were impractical. The teamster did not sit on top of the load; he straddled the roller behind the horses. Photo above taken in camp north of Owen-Withee, and the one below was taken for Wall-Spaulding Lumber Company of Big Falls (Waupaca County). At right, with hand on log, Jack Odell, foreman for W.S.

Decking logs on Menominee Indian Reservation with double-chain technique, early 1900s.

Yawkee-Bissell Lumber Company was picking up small stuff when this picture was taken, in 1920s, north of White Lake. When logs ran small they could be loaded in bunches as seen here. Boom of steam loader hovers over car in center, and at left, engine waits to move train to next landing as soon as logs on skids at right are loaded.

134

Steam hauler, the "Phoenix," made in Eau Claire, is in woods, with stearsman up front to "drive" the bob sleighs. Photo probably from Chippewa Valley.

North West Lumber Company steam hauler in woods near Stanley, Wisconsin. Photo is enlarged from postcard, dated August 5, 1916.

In the 1920s, the Holt caterpiller tractor began to replace steam haulers and horses for hauling logs out of camp to mills or railroad sidings. This one was hauling for Tigerton Lumber Company in camp west of Elcho.

Tigerton Lumber Company, Tigerton, was one of first in Wisconsin to use trucks to haul logs out of woods. Logs on truck appear to be mixed hardwood, not pine. FWD (Four Wheel Drive) is manufactured at Clintonville. Photo dates to early 1930s.

Roddis Lumber & Veneer Company's Climax built at Erie, Pennsylvania by Heisler Locomotive Company, C/N 1477, in 1923, and bought by Roddis from Fountain-Campbell Lumber Company at Ladysmith. Engine seen here has pulp cars in train at Park Falls, where R.L. & V. had veneer plant. Engine was scrapped in 1930s.

Camp and loading yard for Yawkee-Bissell Lumber Company, north of White Lake.

Postcard picture of steam hauler near Athens, probably for Rietbrock Lumber Company. Card is dated September 5, 1911.

Log train emerging from woods bound for sawmill in White Lake operated by Yawkee-Bissell Lumber Company. This 2-6-0 was built in Philadelphia for the Charcoal Iron Company, and purchased by Y-B, who used it until 1947 when it was sold to the Marinette, Tomahawk & Western Railroad. It made its last run in 1957 and was donated to city of Tomahawk for a museum piece. It stands in park at south end of bridge over Wisconsin River on Business 51.

Scene at Hale Mylrea
Camp, Long Lake, Wis

Caption printed on postcard picture, here enlarged, refers to Hale Mylrea's Camp at Long Lake. Mylrea was from Wausau where family had long been associated with lumbering. This Long Lake lies north of Oconto. Hastily-built track and roadbed was typical of logging railways. They were pulled up and laid down according to location of next grove of white pine.

Photo from 1890s probably taken in Waupaca County. Logs are being loaded on Russel cars, not flat cars. Note coupling in car at left. Men on handcar are using handcar for easy conveyance to move up and down track where needed in loading operations. Men at left and right on handcar wore same type of homespun gloves and are probably brothers.

Wisconsin & Northern's #7 at Scott's Siding between Gresham and Neopit. Log pile faintly visible at extreme left where cars have been loaded on siding. Stakes in flat cars suggest picture taken after 1915. John Fowler conductor, and L.G. Guenther, engineer, stand in center.

Chicago & North Western Rail Road built branch line from Conover to Hackley to bring out lumber products of sawmill operated by the Hackley, Phelps & Bonnell Lumber Company. (Hackley was later renamed Phelps). In photo above train skirts Smoke Lake.

Above: Train load of logs probably for Rhinelander sawmills, 1890s. Woman at right stands behind boy next to woodbox.

Left: Saw filer was one of highest paid men in logging camp. Instead of $1 a day, he probably got $1.50, board and room. He is shown here with a portable vise, often taken directly into the woods where the sawyers were falling trees. But his regular place of business is probably the tarpaper shack at back. Here he did most of the saw filing, and here he also had his own bunk apart from the crew. A.J. Kingsbury of Antigo took picture.

A switcher at Wausau pushes train of logs to local sawmill. Postcard picture is post-dated August 24, 1911.

A logging engine, 4-6-0, on the Duluth & South Western near Drummond. Camp buildings stand at right. Photo taken about 1915.

The Shay Engine in Logging Operations

When the small Shay railroad engine was used as the prime mover in logging operations, it was a machine liked by the man at the throttle and by the man in charge of the operations. And there were sound mechanical reasons for this. Although the power of the Shay was derived from steam, its power train bore a strong resemblance to the modern diesel locomotive.

The Shay stood squarely on all wheels and applied power to all of them equally. Moreover, the undercarriage was flexible so that uneven rails were taken in stride, for logging railroads were notoriously rough and uneven.

The early Shay engine's running gear was built much like that of a railroad flat car. Two sets of four wheel trucks bore all the weight, including that of the tender. All wheels were powered, and the undercarriage, to repeat, was flexible.

Power came to the axles by mechanical means, and here we have the similarity to the diesel electric rigs of today. From a twin cylinder upright engine which hung amid ships on the right hand side of the boiler, shafts ran fore and aft, carried on universal joints. Through corner gears these shafts drove the axles upon which the wheels were mounted.

The wheels were usually twenty-four to twenty-six inches. And gear ratio varied between about one and a half to one and two to one. In both cases, the engine ran faster than the wheels.

The reciprocating steam engine is touted for the smooth power it produces, and this is quite true of a mill engine running a couple hundred revolutions per minute with a huge flywheel-pulley. However, at slower speeds with less flywheel, because of the action of a crank and the inherent change in thrust of a reciprocating engine, the power of a side arm driven railroad engine is pulsating at low starting speeds. There are, in the power impulse of the side arm driven engine, four points of low power thrust and four points of high thrust per revolution.

While this has no effect at road speed, it does effect the standing start of a critical load. The wheels will slip during the high thrust, and no engineer can close the throttle fast enough to stop a wild, slipping runaway. He is careful not to open his throttle too much, thereby cutting down on the engine's power and train-starting ability.

A road engine with larger wheels rolls ahead

more than twelve feet per engine revolution. A Shay engine rolled but three or four feet per engine revolution. This let the Shay engine roll a bit faster when starting a load and cut down immensely on thrust fluctuation. Moreover, the engineer could use his power more effectively.

For size, the Shay was a little giant. It sacrificed road speed for starting power. But this made little difference in logging operations because of short hauls and because the road bed was not meant for speedy operations.

The Shay was no match for a road engine out on the high iron. It was never meant to be. In fact, when a Shay was moved in a train on the main line, its drive line had to be disassembled, for road speed was just too much for the engine.

Late model Shay engines were more sophisticated and also larger. They had three cylinder engines and three powered trucks of four wheels, giving a twelve-wheel grip on the rails. An engine of early model would have weighed about the same as a large semi-truck tractor. The top of the fore end of the boiler was only about five feet six inches above the rail. Most Shays were wood burners and therefore economical to use in the woods and around the sawmills. They were easy to operate and maintain.—Allard M. Peterson

Narrow gauge Shay engine operated by Dessert Lumber Company of Mosinee. This is three-cylinder rig which suggests it was built after 1885, but lack of construction number in photograph makes history of engine difficult. It was not used to handle full-sized railroad cars. It has a "pin and link" drawbar and steam brakes. Sand dome was probably added by local blacksmith.

Old boarding house which once catered to crew working in sawmill at Dancy in Marathon County. House stood on north bank of Little Eau Pleine where iron bridge crosses river. Mr. & Mrs. George Altenburg operated boarding house for a time and continued to live there after sawmill closed. Standing between them is their daughter, Vivian (Mrs. Rickford). J.M. Colby of Wausau took postcard picture, here enlarged, postdated 1909.

One of the last and also largest lumber camps built in Wisconsin was this one for the Rib Lake Lumber Company. Referred to as "Camp 2," it was located several miles north of the village of Rib Lake. Log buildings include mess hall, sleeping quarters, horsebarns, and one for the blacksmith and sawfiler.

Logging crew on Menominee Indian Reservation, ca. 1910. Man at right balances crosscut saw used for falling trees, and at right, tool leaning on woodpile is peavey pole used by drivers floating logs probably down West Branch River to Neopit where big Indian mill is located.

The Round Lake Dam

Round Lake Dam lies on the South Fork of the Flambeau River, about half way between Fifield and Woodruff off Highway 70 on the eastern fringe of the Chequamegon National Forest in Price County. But early settlers and loggers in this area referred to it as "the Pike Lake" dam and therein lies a mystery held back from view by the hands of time. There are actually two large lakes here, stretched out north to south, connected by a channel, actually the South Fork of the Flambeau, the southern lake today known as Pike Lake and the northern as Round Lake.

It would appear that in the early period of logging that these two lakes were considered one lake, known to everyone as Pike Lake, and when a dam was built at the outlet, it was naturally called the Pike Lake Dam. But later topographers gave the northern lake a name, "Round Lake," and since it is at this end of the two lakes that the dam lies on, it has since become known to the National Forest Service as "Round Lake Dam."

Built in the early 1880s, the dam was one of the most important logging dams in Wisconsin in the late 19th Century and into the first years of the 20th Century. Logs cut in the forests to the east and northeast around Lac du Flambeau, were floated down to Pike-Round lake and held there until sawmills located farther down the river on the Flambeau in Fifield, and on the Chippewa River at Chippewa Falls, needed the logs.

The Round Lake Dam is the only one left in the entire state of Wisconsin dating to the logging era. It is barely holding its own against the ravages of time, spring floods and winter ice, although what the visitor sees of it today is not entirely original. This would be expecting too much, for it has been restored and repaired from time to time.

But without this dam, early lumbermen could not float their logs to their sawmills. The river level rises and falls, according to natures gifts, and the river is not the same depth everywhere. Some places it widens out and shallows appear. In other places the river runs through rapids—whitewater—which means stones below the surface, or glinting just above the surface, a good place for a log to get snagged, or turned around instead of heading down stream.

Building a dam solved most of these problems. When the drivers, also called "river pigs," were

ready to move a thousand logs or so, down stream, the gates of the dam were closed, and the level of the lake rose several feet to form a "head" of water. When the drivers were ready, the main waste gate was lifted by chains on a winch which then allowed the water to rush under the gate. This went on for several hours and by that time the level of the river below the dam rose one or two feet, sometimes more. When the logs reached a rapids, the rocks below were buried in water, and when the logs reached a shallow, they floated across without impediment.

When the drive started, the logs were actually sent through one or both of the gates located on either side of the waste gate. These were called "sluice gates" because the logs were "sluiced" or passed through time. It is not certain whether both sluice gates on the Round Lake Dam were used at the same time, or whether only one was opened for sluicing. Nor does it appear that anyone ever took a picture of it that survives.

The drivers followed the "drive," as it was called, guiding the logs away from shore and trying to avoid over hanging branches of trees, or large rocks in the center which even the flooded stream could not top. The drivers used a *batteau,* French for "boat," a long, wooden boat, well balanced and propelled by oars or pushed along by long poles. The drivers moved in these batteaux, back and forth across the river, trying to keep the logs moving. Occasionally they would jump on a log and ride it to a danger spot or to get across to the other side, but most of the work was done from the batteaux.

The current carried the logs down stream. The drivers' main job was to prevent a log from catching on a rock or an island in midstream and forming a blockade, called a "jam." If a bunch of logs formed a jam on a rock, or small island, in the center of the river, referred to by the drivers as a "center," it was sometimes possible to find a "key" log and loosen it, a dangerous task under any circumstances, but most log jams ran from shore to shore, sometimes forming a wall of scrambled logs fifteen feet high, running back, that is, upstream, a mile or more. There was no key log in these jams. They were torn apart with dynamite or oxen and horses pulling one log at a time from shore. It often took days, and even weeks to break

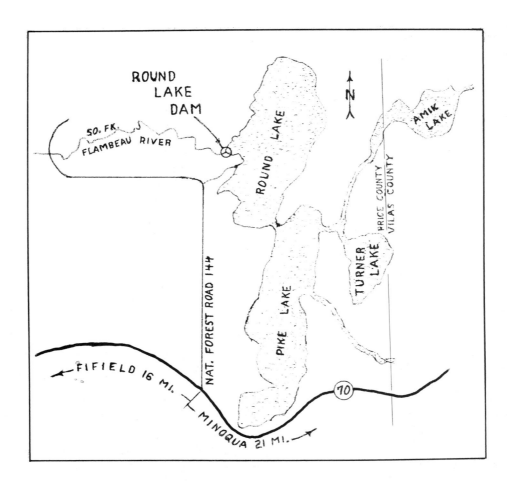

up a jam of this size. Logs kept piling up because there were no telephones to call back to the people on the dam to stop sluicing more logs.

Most rivers had more than one dam. Often a log passed through several dams en route to its destinations. For example, on the Little Wolf River there were twelve dams beginning with the Upper Dam in Marathon County, and running through Portage and Waupaca Counties all the way to the junction of the Little Wolf with the big Wolf below Royalton.

Most dams on the Little Wolf, for example, had two gates, a waste gate and sluice gate, but larger rivers required three gate dams of one type or another. The longest wooden dam in Wisconsin was more than 600 feet long, located on the Chippewa River below the present Holcombe flowage.

In the early years, the Round Lake Dam passed through the hands of several lumber companies as different tracts of timber were sold or exchanged.

In 1906 The Chippewa River & Improvement Company, a subsidiary of Weyerhaeuser industries, sold the rights to the dam to Menasha Wooden Ware Company, manufacturers of wood-

en products such as pails, tubs, barrel staves, water tanks, and in 1909 the last of the big pine logs for Weyerhaeuser were sluiced through the dam.

In 1911 the dam and several forties around it were sold to Otto C. Doering, an officer of Sears, Roebuck & Company of Chicago, who had fallen in love with the dam and the wilderness around it. And it was not until 1915 that Doering got control of the dam from Menasha Wooden Ware. He built several summer lodges around the lake and at least one house with a stone foundation that stood just below the dam. The stonework can still be seen.

In the early 1930s Doering, a conservationist at heart, had the dam rebuilt. He died in 1955 and after his death, his sons, Otto Jr. and Paul, sold the entire estate, including dam, to the United States Forest Service.

Visitors to the dam today can walk across the new plank deck built by Forest Service. The dam is a constant reminder of the great area of logging and lumbering in Wisconsin. It is located in a beautiful setting, surrounded by tall red pines. It should be restored again, and preserved forever.

Peter A. Weiler (Park Falls) stands on deck of Round Lake Dam as it looks today. Waste gate has been raised to allow water from lake to run into Flambeau River. Lake level is maintained by temporary log dam located about 100 feet above dam. Picture below, taken farther down stream, shows gate at right used for sluicing logs. Dam had similar gate at left, barely visible, which in logging era may have been used as an extra sluicing gate but when dam was rebuilt in 1930s, this was made into a fishway. "Cricket," a poodle, stands at right.

Jim Falls (west of Cornell) on Chippewa River was common place for log jam in olden days, but this picture, taken in early 1900s, will never be duplicated. The falls are being buried by huge new hydroelectric dam of Northern States Power Company.

Log driving dam on Little Wolf River about three miles west of Big Falls (Waupaca County) in photo taken by Parks Studio of Iola, ca. 1891. Dam was situated in stone channel which river passes through.

When logs were being floated down river, there were two crews, the "beat" crew which kept ahead with the main drive and guided logs away from rocks and across shallows, and the "rear crew" which followed the beat crew, often several days later, shoving and pulling on logs which had become stranded in bays and among stumps as shown here. Many logs floated ashore in high water and were stranded when the water level went down. These had to be retrieved with oxen or horses. Main tool of the rear crew is not peavey pole, but pike pole as seen in picture. Location of photo uncertain.

A logging crew stops for lunch in the woods near Galloway, 1913. Ed Page sits at left of his son, Milton.

151

Opposite page, giant white pine cut from forest of Menomonee Indian Reservation, shortly after limbs had been removed. Log was loaded on double trucks and hauled to Milwaukee Arena for annual Sports Show where it was used for timber topping competition. Below, Shawano boosters give big tree warm sendoff. James Caldwell (upper left) logging foreman for Menominee Enterprises, holds canthook, while son Alan looks on. Photographer for Green Bay Press Gazette took picture.

Caption at bottom of original photograph reads: "Wunderlich Mill, Elmhurst, 1880." Elmhurst was located about six miles south of Antigo. In 1890s it had two sawmills, a stave mill, a shoemaker shop and store. Photo gives close-up view of "bull-chain" which traveled up "bull-slide," like an escalator, carrying logs to second deck of mill where sawing was done. In foreground is "hot-pond" a body of water kept warm with steam pipes leading from engine room. Logs were stored here temporarily to thaw out and melt snow and debris. But this picture was not taken in 1880. The mill has been abandoned, and Elmhurst is now a ghost town.

Railroad Spurs around Summit Lake

I was the agent at Summit Lake in the heyday of the logging industry and I can recall a number of logging spurs that were located off the main line of the Chicago & North Western between Summit Lake and Elcho. From Deerbrook north, I can name Honcik Siding, which was also the junction of the Ormsby line and Kroms Spur, Kempster and Miller's Spur just south of the bridge across the west branch of the Eau Claire River on present County Trunk B.

For a time there was a spur to the east of Millers Spur where the Wisconsin Timber and Land Company loaded out forest products for several years.

Then there was Koepenich at the junction of the branch that ran to Pearson. Up to 1920 this track terminated at Hoboken Lake, one mile east of Koepenich. After World War I, several logging operations began between Koepenich and Pearson which called for rail extensions and more spurs. The spur at Hoboken Lake was called Lake Spur. Beyond that lay Kellogg Spur, Mortenson Spur, in Section 15, and three C.W. Fish Lumber Company spurs, all told more than twelve.

About 1925, the Langlade Lumber Company finished their operations on the Bass Lake line and moved their camps to Pearson. This resulted in a further extension of track east and southeast toward Bryant. There was a regular Pearson run out of Antigo daily to handle this spur. Jack Warren was the conductor most of the time. The billing was all done at Summit Lake station and we were running about twenty carloads of logs daily.

The Bass Lake Line junction which was located a mile or more south of Summit Lake, called for a crew out of Antigo twice daily to handle the twenty to forty cars of forest products. John Romeis and Jack McIenna were the main conductors. The billings were made over the Bass Lake telephone and ready for the crew when they got here with the loads.

The Langlade Lumber Company had three locomotives hauling logs out of the woods over 40 miles of trackage which linked their timber holdings west of Summit Lake. At the peak of operations in World War I, the company had a thousand men getting out the timber. The company had "men catchers" in the big cities recruiting lumberjacks to work in the woods. For a time there was a special coach on the Limited train No. 11 out of Chicago that set out at Summit Lake, full of woodsmen. One man was in charge and at day break he marched his little army of troops down to Bass Lake where they boarded a logging train and were taken to one of the camps in the area. Henry Higgins of Antigo was one of the "men catchers." Recruiting for the labor force also went on in the Duluth and the Twin Cities. The new hands got their free railway ticket but they had to bring their own "turkey" (bag or suitcase), and these were checked through for them, lest they hop off the train before they got here. Many of these city workers did not have what it takes to work in the woods and were soon dismissed.

When the U.S. entered World War I in 1917, many of the lumberjacks were drafted for military duty and the company had to find replacements for them, many of whom were newcomers who could hardly speak English. Some were not accustomed to woods work and got hurt, mostly with the axe, and they were shipped to Antigo to see the doctor, some with blood running out of their boots.

When the Langlade Lumber Company took over the timber lands of the Paine Lumber Company (Oshkosh) in 1916, they added more trackage to cover their newly-acquired timber lands. All the grading was done by hand under contractors Peppard & Burril of Minneapolis. This company built a camp for a crew of sixty Swedes who did the grading with shovel, grub hoes and wheelbarrows. The work was set up in stations which had so much grading to be done in cubic yards, at so much a station. They were hard workers, these Swedes, and made good money for those days. Now and then they hit town for a weekend of boozing but they were never a problem for the local authorities.

Bass Lake was started as a camp about 1890 by Henry Shultz and his brother Ed, jobbers for Paine Lumber Company. After logging off the timber around Bass Lake, they built Camp 1 on Long Lake (now called Deep Woods Lake) and logged that off. Sam Brown, a brother-in-law of Schultz, built Camp 3 on Kettle Hole Lake outlet, about 1894. He landed logs on Kettle Lake and built a dam and dug a channel so that he could sluice his logs into Deep Woods Lake, and load on the south end of the lake. Some of the men used the

Postcard picture, enlarged, of North West Lumber Company sawmill at Owen, ca. 1910.

dam for water power to turn the gridstone to sharpen their axes.

About 1898, Jim O'Brien built Camp 2 on Bullhead Lake and took off the pine in that area. By that time, the Bass Lake spur extended to Camp 2, but Paine had only one locomotive.

About 1900 Camp 4 was built on Dynamite Lake and the spur was extended to this camp. Dave Jackson was the first woods boss here and he was followed by George Durler. The logs were decked on Dynamite Lake during the winter and a chain hoist took the logs out of the lake and up a slide onto bunk-and-chain (Russel) cars and shipped to Oshkosh where Paine had its main sawmill.

Lou Filyes was walking boss for Paine until the company was taken over by Langlade Lumber Company. Dave Edick, head cruiser, lived at the Bass Lake boarding house. I recall two other cruisers, Fred Kalkofen and Charles Bacon.

Sam Lawrence, a private logger, took the pine around Hunting River and landed it on the north branch of the river. From here he had his drivers float the logs over a series of dams all the way to the mouth of the Wolf River. The clearing on the south side of Summit Lake is named "Lawrence Clearing," because he used this to graze his oxen in summer.

Robert Saering was one of the lumbermen who used the Summit Lake siding for shipping lumber out. He had a sawmill and a farm at East Upham. And about a mile north of Summer Lake lay a spur for Tigerton Lumber Company, a company which logged for several years around Pine Lake west of Elcho. They brought in a steam hauler to bring their logs to the railway for shipping out to their mill in Tigerton. Charlie Kannenberg was woods boss.

A mile or more north of Summit Lake lay the Interlake Pulp & Paper Company's spur. This company used a "drop landing" to load their logs. The bank along the spur was high enough so that the men could run skids out and over the car and roll the logs or pulpwood directly into the gondola, that is, dropping them into the gondola without using a jammer, and that's how the name "drop landing" came to be.

Kellogg Lumber company logged a few years at the spur about two miles north of Summit Lake.

Summit Lake was at the top of Monico Hill. We had a big yard here where the hill crew could set out their train and go back for another trip. There was a regular hill crew tied up at Monico. In fact, most of the crews lived there. Jim Farley was the conductor for many years. When he passed on

Fred McGlone took his place.

The Pratt Line crew generally came over the hill after making their run to Parrish and Harrison. About all they could handle was eight to ten loads. They had only a small standard locomotive. The Crandon crew also made trips on the hill from Pelican.

Mike Garrit was the conductor on the Pratt Line for many years, and Cliff Williams, Monty Beard and Jim Chadek were conductors on the Crandon Line. During World War I business was heavy and as many as five hill crews were required to keep the hill clear of loads. There was a freight crew daily from Antigo to Watersmeet and another out of Watersmeet to Antigo, plus a regular switch crew from Antigo to Monico and return. In addition there were regular time freights 281 and 282 Antigo-to-Ashland both ways.

In this early period, cars had the old draft timbers and many draw bars were pulled out and car repair crews had to be sent to Summit Lake almost daily to make repairs. We also had passenger trains No. 14 southbound around 6:15 a.m. This crew came back on No. 4 around 10:00 p.m. Conductor Bettie Sr., had this run for years, followed by Harry Jennings.

I also had passenger train No. 16 due in Summit Lake around 11:30 a.m. and No. 17 around 1:00 p.m., plus Limiteds No. 12 around midnight and

No. 11 around 3:00 a.m. Travel on No. 17 was generally so heavy that the conductor could barely pick up all the tickets out of Antigo before he got to Summit Lake. Conductors on trains 16, 17, 12 and 11 took these runs on week days and the following week nights. Conductors I recall include Brown, Hall, Riley, Quinland, Kelly and Fenn. —Peter Rasmussen Sr.

Postcard picture, enlarged, taken about 1915.

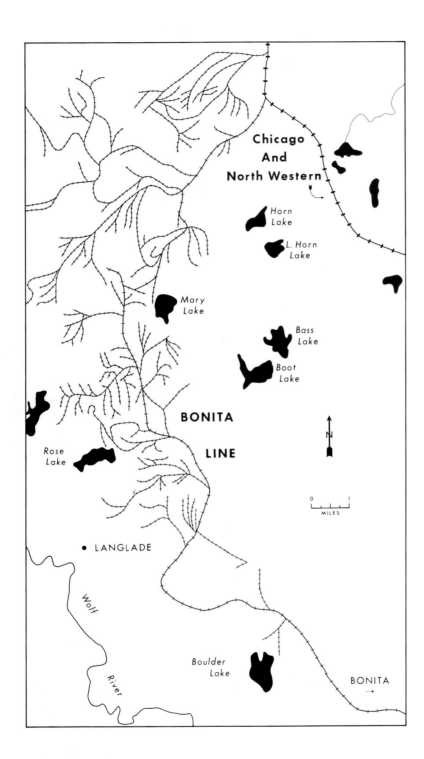

Bonita Logging Line, often called the "Cucumber Line," was begun in 1916 in southeast Langlade County. While most of the pine was harvested, there remained good stands of hardwoods and this timber was moved by rail to the sawmills of the Holt Lumber Company, and the Oconto Company in Oconto. The railroad best suited to haul the logs was the Gillette to Wabeno line of the Chicago & North Western. A branch was built from Bonita in Oconto County into Langlade County, then north to about the middle of the east line of Town 32, Range 14 East. Trackage on the Bonita line was laid down and when one stand of timber was harvested, the tracks were picked up and laid into another stand of timber. Portions of the roadbeds remain in addition to bits of bridge footings, trestles, and clearings where logging camps were once located. Part of the road beds now serve snowmobilers on the one-time "Cucumber line."—Map courtesy of Randall E. Rohe.

A modified wood burner, sunflower stack, made by Porter Locomotive Works, hauling logs to mill, probably near Chippewa Falls for Chippewa Lumber & Boom Company, some time in 1890s. Girl holds puppy. Note link pin above step board, and pile of slabwood at right.

Saw Mill, Marinette, Wis.

Picture of sawmill at Marinette enlarged from postcard.

Giant load of tanbark (peeled elm bark), so called because the juice of the bark, after processing in a tannery, was used for tanning hides and leather. There were several tanneries in the Chippewa Valley in early 1900s. Load here was probably going to Phillips. Large loads of bark could be hauled but this one is an outsize load for benefit of cameraman. Note hook under tongue. Chain ran forward to another team of horses in the lead.

Holt & Balcom Lumber Company, Camp 1, at Lakewood (on Highway 32 northeast of White Lake). Often called "Depot Camp," it was built in 1881 and is oldest camp on original location in Wisconsin. Road along McCaslin Brook was used to bring in supplies from Oconto and for lumberjacks using Shanks Mare while looking for work in the woods. Building is "dingle" type, kitchen and eating area at left, bunk room at right, separated by "dingle," an open space between the two buildings but roofed over, often used for storage. Building was restored by Lakewood Lions Club under direction of Francis Pinkowsky, and is open to tourists on weekends in summer months.

Paul Peterson, Antigo, had own means of transportation, a velocipede. He served as camp cook in woods near Laona.

161

All the loneliness of a home on the cut-over lands of northern Wisconsin seems reflected in this picture taken of the abandoned farm (left) of John F. Dietz, "Defender of Cameron Dam on Thornapple River." Picture was taken in 1910 after arrest of Dietz for the murder of Oscar Harp, a sheriff's deputy, killed in line of duty while creeping down from lumberpiles (upper left) toward barn where Dietz was shooting from hay loft. Dietz family hid inside log house (center) protecting themselves against hail of bullets fired by posse intent on capturing Dietz. In distance at right stand two log shanties used by log drivers for Chippewa Lumber & Boom Company. Cameron dam (not visible) stood at left of shanties. Snow-covered swamp in foreground shows road probably used by Dietz family to drive to Winter. Swamp was once covered by pond created by dam. Thornapple River, not visible, runs below hill, roughly north to south at this point. Buildings were later destroyed in forest fires and dam washed out except for embankments which are still intact, covered with trees and brush.

A Chronology of "Firsts" in Wisconsin Forest History

1809—First sawmill built by Jacob Franks, on the Fox River near present-day DePere.

1819—First sawmill west of Green Bay, built by Colonel Daniel Shaw on the Black River near Black River Falls.

1822—First timber cutting permit issued in the Chippewa River Valley, by U.S. Indian Agent James H. Lockwood.

1828—First marketing of wild cranberries, by Daniel Whitney, via boat from the mouth of the Yellow River near Necedah to Galena, Illinois.

1830—First native forest animal to become extinct was the buffalo.

1831—First sawmill on the Menominee River, built by William Farnsworth and Charles R. Brush.

—First sawmill on the Red Cedar River, built by Lockwood and Rolette at Menomonie.

—First sawmill on the Wisconsin River, built by Daniel Whitney at Point Basse (now Nekoosa).

1837—First known permission given by Indians to white men to cut timber and build sawmills in the St. Croix River Valley.

—First sawmill on the Chippewa River, built by Jean Brunet and H.L. Dousman near Chippewa Falls.

1839—First fleet of lumber sawed in the St. Croix River Valley, by the Marine Lumber Company, on the Minnesota side of the St. Croix River.

1840—First fleet of lumber rafts went down the Wisconsin River from the Francis Biron sawmill at Biron.

—First general use made of the mechanically-operated muley saw.

1841—First law enacted regulating construction of dams on navigable rivers for log-driving purposes.

1842—First rafting of logs, done by Mormons on the Black River, to their settlement at Nauvoo, Illinois, on the Mississippi River.

1848—First paper mill, built at Milwaukee by Ludington and Garland, to make newsprint from rag stock.

—First towing of log rafts by steam towboats, on the St. Croix River.

1876—First reforestation project, completed by Walter Ware near Hancock by the transplanting of wild stock with oxen-drawn wagons.

1878—First state park lands established comprising 50,000 acres in Iron and Vilas counties.

1881—First steam-powered logging railroad, the Crescent Springs Railroad operated by the Shell Lake Lumber Company, Washburn County.

—First strike of sawmill workers at Eau Claire Lumber Company, Eau Claire, Wisconsin.

1883—First veneer plant established by Frost Veneer Company near Antigo.

1884—First plywood plant established by F. Eggers Company at Two Rivers.

—First wood pulp mill built by Pioneer Pulp Company at Centralia (Wisconsin Rapids) on Wisconsin River.

1887—First integrated pulp and paper mill begins operations after converting old sawmill into Centralia Pulp & Water Power Company.

1892—First official observance of Arbor Day in Wisconsin.

1895—First formal forest protection organization adopted by state legislature.

1898—Tom Fleming of Eau Claire becomes first in Wisconsin to win world championship log rolling competition.

1900—First comprehensive forestry law passed to create Forestry Commission.

—First resident instruction in forestry offered at University of Wisconsin.

1913—First forest plantation started near Star Lake in Vilas County using seedlings grown in first state tree nursery.

1915—First aerial forest patrol flight, made by Jack Vilas from the Trout Lake state forest headquarters, marking the first time anywhere that an aircraft was used for detecting and locating forest fires.

1924—First forestry consulting firm, Banzhaf & Watson, organized in Milwaukee.

—First selective logging undertaken, by the Holt Lumber Company of Oconto, under the supervision of Banzhaf & Watson, on 80 acres near Archibald Lake in Oconto County.

1925—First state forest established (Northern Highland State Forest, Vilas County), following the adoption in 1924 of a second forestry amendment to the state constitution.

—First reforestation program by a public utility, initiated by the Wisconsin Power & Light Co. in cooperation with George Crandall, in the Wisconsin Dells area.

—First industrial forester, F.G. Kilp, hired by the Nekoosa-Edwards Paper Company, who then began the first industrial forestry program in the Lake States with the establishment of his company's tree nursery.

—First authorization given by the state to the federal government to purchase land within the state for national forest purposes.

1926—First joint agreement made between the University of Wisconsin and the Wisconsin Conservation Department to initiate a program of better forestry and land use among private forest landowners.

—First farm forestry extension program begun, with F.G. Wilson as the first extension forester.

1927—First forest land tax relief legislation enacted with the passage of the Forest Crop Law.

—First enabling legislation passed permitting school districts and municipalities to own land for, and engage in, forestry programs.

—First meeting of the new Wisconsin Conservation Commission held, with William Mauthe of Fond du Lac as its first chairman.

1928—First county forest established under County Forest Reserve Law, in Langlade County.

—First state forestry conference, held in Milwaukee, brought together all forestry interests to review past accomplishments and to develop policies for the ensuing 25 years.

—First tract of land acquired by the U.S.

Arbor Vitae was once a big mill town located north of Woodruff. Mill stood on shore of lake. This view is enlarged from postcard.

Forest Service to form the beginning of the Nicolet National Forest: 12,940 acres near Three Lakes, purchased from the Thunder Lake Lumber Company of Rhinelander.

—First school forests established by the Laona and Crandon school districts as a result of enabling legislation enacted in 1927.

1930—First cooperative fire control agreement between an industrial forest landowner and the Wisconsin Conservation Department entered into by the Nekoosa-Edwards Paper Company.

1933—First two federal Civilian Conservation Corps camps in Wisconsin constructed on the Nicolet National Forest near Eagle River and Three Lakes.

—First rural zoning ordinance in the nation adopted by Oneida County, subsequently becoming a model for other counties in Wisconsin and throughout the United States.

1944—First conservation education program begun by Trees-for-Tomorrow, Inc., with the financial support of nine paper companies and the cooperation of the U.S. Forest Service in making available its training school facilities at Eagle River.

1946—First "farm foresters" appointed by the Wisconsin Conservation Department to assist farm woodland owners.

1947—First forest tract, owned and managed by a group of newspaper publishers and editors, established as the Wisconsin Press Association Forest near Eagle River; also the first and only such a demonstration forest nationally.

1948—First purchases made of tree-planting machines by members of the Wisconsin Bankers Assocation for use by private land owners, in cooperation with county forestry departments and Trees-for-Tomorrow.

1950—First statewide forest inventory began as a cooperative effort between state, federal, county and industrial forestry organizations.

—First forest entomologist, Norbert Underwood, employed by the Wisconsin Conservation Department.

1951—First aerial forest insect control project by a private forest landowner conducted by the Mosinee Paper Mills Company, in Douglas County, to combat a major infestation of the jack pine tussock moth.

1955—First tree farmer registered in Wisconsin under the national tree farm program sponsored by American Forest Products Industries, Inc.: Bruce Buell, near Green Bay.

1970—First satellite debarking plant, for the production of peeled aspen pulpwood, built by the J.C. Campbell Company of Duluth, Minnesota, at Mercer.

1972—First satellite roundwood chipping plant, for the production of debarked aspen chips for pulping purposes, built by Lake States Enterprises of Bemidji, Minnesota, at Ashland.

1976—First association for the preservation of Wisconsin's forest history organized, with Thomas A. Fulk, supervisor of the Nicolet National Forest as its first president.

1977—First school forest certified as a tree farm by the American Forest Institute under revised rules of eligibility: Wausau School Forest of 800 acres.

1979—First association of private non-industrial woodland owners organized, with Ernest Brickner of Whitehall as its first president.

—First waferboard plant constructed by Louisiana-Pacific Corporation at Hayward.

—First modern public school, Park Falls High School, equipped with a wood-fired heating plant in conjunction with a conventional gas-fired unit, began operations utilizing wood wastes, sawdust, bark and chips for fuel.

1980—First utility to generate electricity by burning chips, sawdust and bark, the Lake Superior District Power Company at Ashland, began producing 20 million kilowatts annually.

—First seeding of hardwoods by helicopter in the United States, done by the Department of Natural Resources on the Flambeau River State Forest near Winter.—

—Compiled by Frank Fixmer for FOREST HISTORY ASSOCIATION newsletter "Chips and Sawdust."

When oxen needed to be shoed, they were trussed up in stanchion with belly-band to lift feet off ground. Belly band was tightened by winch. Note hole in pole for bar, and chains around pole. Oxen do not have stability of a horse and cannot stand on three feet without losing balance. But they were mainstay of logging woods throughout 18th and 19th Centuries in America, and were used both on the haul, and for skidding logs out of forest. After 1900 horses replaced oxen.

Glossary of Logging Terms

Bad Chance—a tract of scattered timber, difficult to get at and a risk for buyer or jobber.

Bark jumper,—*see* jumper.

Barn Boss—one who supervised care of horses and chores around barn or stable.

Batteau—long rowboat used on river drives, originally French.

Beadle—a foreman.

Buckers—two men with crosscut saw who sawed fallen tree into lengths of sixteen feet or less.

Bull chain—a heavy chain which held logs on clamps while ascending to second floor of sawmill on bull slide.

Bull cook—an assistant in kitchen who carried wood, swept floors and helped with dishes, In early 1900s bull cook also was a helper around crew loading logs.

Bull slide—ramp leading from mill pond to second deck of sawmill used for conveying logs into mill.

Bunk—cross pieces on sleigh on which logs rested.

Bunk camp—early name for logging camp, usually where both kitchen and sleeping quarters were in one building.

Center—logs stranded in midstream on rock or sandbar.

Chainer—man who hooked chains around log to evener, or to oxen yokes.

Checker—a latter day expression referring to a man who counts pulp footage or other piece work.

Chopper—a man who once chopped trees down with an ax.

Chore boy—another term for bull cook.

Chute—*see* slough

Contractor—same as jobber, a person who contracts to cut a given number of board feet of logs for a lumber company or private operator.

Cook-ee—assistant or second cook.

Corner-bind—a special piece of chain with fid hook used to secure or bind first tier of logs to sleigh bunks at the four corners.

Cutting chance—*see* good chance or bad chance.

Deacon seat—a long bench in front of bunkbeds for men to sit on.

Deck—any flat surface either on the ground, in a mill, or on top of load of logs.

Dingle—storage space between sleeping shanty and cook shanty under roof.

Drive—a noun meaning a raft or collection of logs being guided downriver by crew of "drivers."

Dry roll—logs stranded some distance from river were rolled back to river by horses, one on either end of log with swivels.

Good chance—a tract of timber which should make money for the buyer or contractor.

Fid hook—oval or flat hook used on corner bind.

Godevil—a v-shaped crouch cut from tree, or made by blacksmith on which one end of log rested for skidding.

Head of water—water held back at dam to be released when sluicing of logs through dam begins.

Head mogul—a lumber company representative or officer.

Head sawyer—man who held lever which controlled action of saw carriage in sawmill.

High rear—logs hung up on river banks in rear of drive.

Hog—one who drove logs on river.

Hookers—two men who handled pup-hooks in loading operations.

Hot pond—enclosed area in pond below sawmill where water was kept warm in winter by exhaust from boiler room.

Jackstaff—flag pole and pole for "nighthawk" on bow of river steamboats.

Jobber—*see* contractor.

Jumper—a bob sleigh with two runners used to haul supplies or lunch through woods before roads were brushed out.

Kerf—slice in a log made by circular or crosscut saw.

Landing—any place along a river, or railroad siding, where logs were temporarily decked before loading on flat cars, or rolled into river for drive to mill.

Lead team—two horses ahead of team hitched to

down on the jackstaff of a river boat to aid pilots in navigation.

Piss wagon—a wooden water tank on sleigh runners used for icing logging roads.

Punkrot—an ulcer in the bark of a tree which often indicated inner decay.

Push—a camp foreman or strawboss.

Rampike—a spike of dead tree with no branches.

Rank—an extended pile of hemlock bark, or cordwood pulp.

Road monkey—anyone who kept logging road free of manure or debris.

Rollway—logs decked several yards high, usually on a river embankment pending spring drive to sawmill.

Running drive—a drive of logs on river where no

This is a "landing," or place where logs were brought to and decked into piles as seen at right. Load of logs on sleigh at left has come in from woods and is being unloaded. Crew in center is "tailing down" (rolling) the logs on skid-poles to create another pile where logs will be stored until spring. Skid-poles in foreground and logs on load appear to be hardwood and not all of same quality. Note hollow butts in pile at right. Crew was probably working for Kaiser Lumber Company of Eau Claire which had several camps in Sawyer County in early 1900s cleaning up the hardwood after the pine was harvested by earlier companies. Logs shown here were probably shipped by train to company mill in Eau Claire.

evener on sleigh.

Logger—anyone who contracts to cut trees and deliver them to sawmill or to a landing.

Lumberjack—anyone who worked in a logging camp, sawmill, millyard or a railroad siding, a term not heard until after 1890s.

Muzzle-loader—a bunk bed in sleeping shanty which could only be entered from one end, as opposed to "side-loader" which could be entered from open side of bunk running parallel to wall.

Nighthawk—a metal ball which slid up and

attempt is made to retrieve strays, all effort being expended on getting as many logs as possible downriver in shortest time.

Rutter—a wooden device pulled by team of horses to create ruts in snow sprayed with water at night to create iced roads.

Sacking—wading into a river to get logs stranded on sandbars or rocks back into river current.

Sawyers—men who sawed trees down, mostly after 1890 when crosscut saw replaced ax for falling trees.

Scaler—anyone who measured the board feet of

lumber in a log or on boards coming off saw.

Shanty boy—a term heard in 19th Century, mostly in Michigan, occasionally in Wisconsin, for anyone working in the woods—a lumberjack.

Skidding—pulling a log on the ground behind a team of horses.

Skidding teamster—one who drove team bringing logs out of woods to road, usually with skidding tong or on godevil.

Slough—water behind an island on a river separated from main channel.

Sluice—to run logs through a gate on a river dam.

Sluiceway—a gate for sluicing logs through dam.

Snowsnake—mythical creatures, second cousin to the Hodag.

Smithy—camp blacksmith.

Straw boss—any boss of small crew, or assistant to foreman.

Swamper—lowest man on the totem, usually worked with crew in woods, clearing brush away for skidding teamster, or limbing trees on ground, or hooking chain around log to team.

Tailing down—rolling a log on skids with cant-hook to point where logs could be picked up by jammer, or on cross-haul.

Top loader—man on top of load of logs, or on deck of logs who guided upcoming logs into place with canthook.

Tote road—any narrow road brushed out of woods wide enough for a team and sleigh to bring supplies to camp.

Tote team—team of horses used for bringing supplies to camp.

Towhead—an island with a low bluff, or point at upper end.

Turkey—a bag or sack used by lumberjacks to carry personal effects and clothing.

Walker—*see* walking boss.

Walking boss—a foreman of several camps who either rode or walked from one camp to the other to supervise operations.

Wanigan—a boat with kitchen facilities either under a canvas top, or wood shack; also a small store in camp where personal necessities could be purchased, and tobacco.

Windfall—any dead tree lying in the woods.

Fiber Mill, Kaukauna, Wis.

Fiber mill was early name often given to paper mill. This photo is enlarged from postcard, early 1900s.

A "drop landing," seldom seen anywhere else in Wisconsin, was used by Holt Lumber Company for log loading near Oconto. Logs were loaded on railway cars directly from landing but technique was complicated compared with simple horse jammer or steam hoist.

Wing—a collection of logs along shore of river, sometimes impeding log drive, at other times purposely created to divert water into narrow river channel.

Woods boss—a foreman.

Wood-Butcher—camp carpenter who repaired equipment, made canthook handles and maintained buildings.

With barely enough snow on the ground for good sleighing, this steam hauler arrives at a landing with long train of logs, no doubt last of the season, stearman seated up front behind wheel. Photo from Chippewa Valley in camp near Ladysmith.

Load of pine logs has been selected for size and beauty, since no collection of logs, running scale, would be this perfect. The number "7000" is printed on top log to give number of board feet of lumber represented in load. Horses at left were probably "cross-haul" team which loaded logs with single chain technique, and team at right has "hausers" over hames to protect collars from snow and moisture. Leaning on canthook at right is Robert Pugmire, woods boss for Lindsay & Hatten Lumber Company of Manawa, but photo was taken in logging woods north of Galloway, February 10, 1897.

PICTURE CREDITS

5, Portage County Historical Society (hereafter cited as PCHS); 6, Walter Barnsdale Jr. and author collection; 7, State Historical Society of Wisconsin (hereafter cited as SHS); 8, SHS; 9, SHS and Walter Barnsdale Jr.; 10, author; 11, author and SHS; 12, Walter Zeit; 13, PCHS; 14, Walter Raymond; 15, SHS and author; 16, author and Viola Anderson; 17, Peter Rasmussen Sr.; 18, Donna Quinn; 19, Stella Peterson; 20-21, author; 22-23, Walter Barnsdale Jr.; 24-41, Barnsdale Collection PCHS; 43-55, author; 57-61, SHS; 62, SHS and author; 63, Mildred Hagen and Edward P. Dobbe; 64, SHS; 65, SHS; 66, Barnsdale Collection PCHS; 67, author; 68, PCHS and Harry Curran; 69, Scott McCormick; 71, Letitia Caldwell; 72, Walter Barnsdale Jr.; 73, Walter Raymond and PCHS; 74, Stella Peterson; 75, Walter Raymond and Ed Curtis; 76, Walter Raymond; 77-78, author; 79, SHS; 80-81 Marathon County Historical Society (hereafter as MCHS); 82, Langlade County Historical Society (hereafter as LCHS); 83, Letitia Caldwell; 84, author and Gerald Johnson; 85, author; 86-87 MCHS; 88, author; 89, PCHS; 90, author; 91, MCHS; 92-93, Isabel Martin; 94, author; 96, Earl Olson; 98, Walter Zeit and PCHS; 99, PCHS; 100, SHS; 102, Robert Cable; 103, Walter Raymond; 104, Walter Zeit and author; 105, David Jankoski and Gerald Johnson; 106, A.P. Dobbe; 107, SHS; 108, author photo; 110-115, Elwyn West; 116, Leonard Larson; 117, author photo; 119, Anne Kyle; 120-121, Anne Kyle; 122-123, Roland Ziegler; 124, author and SHS; 125, MCHS and Dolores Beaudette; 127, Isabel Martin and Dolores Beaudette; 128, David Jankoski; 130, SHS; 131, Mildred Hagen; 132 LCHS; 133, David Jankoski and author; 134, Letitia Caldwell and White Lake Lumber Company; 135, author and David Jankoski; 136, author and Tigerton Lumber Company; 137, author and White Lake Lumber Company; 138, David Jankoski and White Lake Lumber Company; 139, author; 140, SHS; 141, author; 142, author and Peter Rasmussen Sr.; 143, David Jankoski and Gene Goodwin; 145, author; 146, Harry Curran and Letitia Caldwell; 148, Peter Weiler map; 149, author photos; 150, author; 151, SHS and author; 152-153, Letitia Caldwell; 154, LCHS; 156-157, David Jankoski; 158, Randall Rohe; 159, SHS and David Jankoski; 160, author; 161, George Growell and Ed Curtis; 162-165, author; 167, author and Gerald Johnson; 169, SHS; 170, David Jankoski; 171-172, author.

INDEX